GW00503782

Rock Climbing in Ireland

Rock climbing in Ireland

Edited by Calvin Torrans and Dawson Stelfox

Constable London

First published in Great Britain 1984
by Constable and Company Ltd
10 Orange Street London WC2H 7EG
Copyright © 1984 by Calvin Torrans
and Dawson Stelfox
ISBN 0 09 465320 8
Set in Times 9pt by
Inforum Ltd, Portsmouth
Printed in Great Britain by
The Pitman Press, Bath

This guide is dedicated to all Irish climbers who have given their lives to the mountains, and in particular to those below who, being connected with the editors, played their part in the preparation of this guide.

Sé Billane, who died after an abseiling accident at Fair Head.

Tom Hand, who was lost in a fall from the descent of Artesonraju in the Cordillera Blanca, 1980.

Tommy Maguire, who died of injuries received in a fall on the descent of Bhagarathi II, Garwhal Himalaya, 1981.

Philomena Gilmore, who drowned in February 1982 trying to save the life of a student while instructing a party on a small coastal crag in the Mournes.

Angela Taylor, who died in 1982, after being knocked off the descent from the Aiguille de Peigne by another falling climber.

Contents

	List of illustrations and diagrams	9
	Acknowledgements	14
	Map of rock-climbing areas in Ireland	15
	Introduction	16
	Notes on using the guide	16
	Metric conversion table	18
	Travelling to, and in, Ireland	19
	Maps	19
	Accommodation	19
	Mountain rescue	20
	Bibliography	20
1	Dalkey Quarry, Dublin	23
2	Glendalough, Wicklow	46
3	Luggala, Wicklow	66
4	Coumshingaun, Comeragh Mts, Waterford	82
5	Ailladie, Clare	93
6	Monastir Sink, Fermanagh	106
7	Tormore Crag, Sligo	111
8	Muckros Head, Donegal	123
9	Sail Rock, Donegal	129
10	Malinbeg, Donegal	131
11	Lough Belshade, Donegal	139
12	Lough Barra, Donegal	147
13	Fair Head, Antrim	157
14	Ballygalley Head	195
	Introduction to the Mourne Mts, Co. Down	205
15	Lower Cove, Mourne Mts	208
16	Slieve Beg, Mourne Mts	215
17	Annalong Buttress, Mourne Mts	223
18	Hare's Castle, Mourne Mts	225
19	Spellack, Mourne Mts	229
20	Bernagh Slabs, Mourne Mts	235
21	Pigeon Rock Mountain, Mourne Mts	237
22	Eagle Mountain, Mourne Mts	247
	Index of routes by area	251

Illustrations and diagrams

	Ireland – the climbing areas	15
	1 Dalkey Quarry	
	Area diagram	22
1/1–1/20	West Valley, looking north towards Dublin	24
1/5–1/12	West Valley	26
1/12	Gargoyle Groove	30
1/16	Jameson Ten	32
1/21	Central Buttress	33
1/22–1/26	Upper Cliffs and Tower Ridge	34
1/24	Giant's Staircase (*photo* C. Sheridan)	37
1/25	Graham Crackers	38
1/28–1/30	Upper Cliffs – White Wall	40
1/32–1/36	East Valley, east side	43
	2 Glendalough	
	Area diagram	47
2/0	Twin Buttress from valley path (*photo* E. Goulding)	48
2/1–2/2	Cracks on the Garden of Eden and Expectancy (*photo* E. Goulding)	50
2/3–2/8	West Wing of Twin Buttress (*photo* E. Goulding)	53
2/3	Quartz Gully (*photo* K. Higgs)	54
2/7–2/8	Spillikin Ridge and Sarcophagus	56
2/8	Sarcophagus (*photo* K. Higgs)	58
2/9–2/14	East Wing of Twin Buttress (*photo* E. Goulding)	61
2/15–2/17	Upper Cliffs of Glendalough (*photo* E. Goulding)	62
2/11	Aisling Arête	64
	3 Luggala	
	Area diagram	67
3/0	Crag from lakeside approach path	68
3/1–3/7	Creag Fasra, Luggala	70
3/8–3/11	Main Face, Luggala	72
3/6	Muskrat Ramble	74
3/8	Pine Tree Buttress (*photo* U. MacPherson)	77

3/10	Spearhead (*photo* O. Jacob)	78
3/12	Dance of the Tumblers (*photo* K. Higgs)	81

4 Coumshingaun

	Area diagram	83
4/1–4/3	North-facing cliff (*photo* S. Gallwey)	84
4/2	Dark Angel (*photo* O. Jacob)	86
4/4–4/6	East-facing cliff (*photo* S. Gallwey)	88
4/4	Jabberwock (*photo* H. O'Brien)	91

5 Ailladie

	Crag diagram	92
5/1–5/5	Long Ledge Wall	94
5/7–5/10	Aran Wall	97
5/1	Ground Control	98
5/6	Rollerball (*photo* K. Higgs)	100
5/7	Gallows Pole	102
5/11–5/13	Mirror Wall and The Ramp (*photo* K. Higgs)	103
5/13	The Ramp (*photo* K. Higgs)	105

6 Monastir Sink

	Area diagram	106
6/1–6/2	Left wall	107
6/3	Monastir Direct	108

7 Tormore Crag

	Area diagram	113
7/1–7/5	Left-hand wall of crag	112
7/9–7/13	Right-hand wall and Landmark Boulder	116
7/3	Warthog (*photo* K. Higgs)	118
7/12	Hawk (*photo* K. Higgs)	121

8 Muckros Head

	Area diagram – Malinbeg, Sail Rock and Muckros Head	122
	Detail – Malinbeg and Muckros Head	124
8/4–8/10	Looking back along the tidal platform	125

8/10   Primula (*photo* E. Goulding)   127

9 Sail Rock
9/1   Sail Rock and Main Mast   130

10 Malinbeg
10/5   Moby Dick   132
10/6   The Bold Princess Royal   134
10/9–10/10 Flying Enterprise and Fiddler's Green   136

11 Lough Belshade
            Area diagram – Lough Belshade and Lough
            Barra   140
11/1–11/4   Main face   141
11/0   Right-hand buttress, Upper Tier   143
11/3   Lest We Forget   144

12 Lough Barra
12/0   View from road above farmhouse   146
12/2   Triversion (*photo* A. McQuoid)   148
12/3–12/7   The Delta Face   150
12/7   Tarquin's Groove (*photo* J. Fox)   154

13 Fair Head
            Area diagram   158
13   Wall left of Grey Man's Path   161
13   Grey Man's Path area   162
13/5   Hurricane   164
13/6   Toby Jug   166
13/13   Born to Run (*photo* E. Cooper)   168
13/16–13/17 An Gobán Saor and An Bealach Rhunda   170
13/18–13/22 Main wall from Vandals to Roaring Meg   172
13/23–13/28 Main wall from Conchubair to Salange   174
13/21   Roaring Meg (*photo* K. Higgs)   176
13/25   Mizzen Star (*photo* E. Goulding)   178
13/29–13/34 Left wall of Ballycastle descent gully   180
13/33   Girona   182

13/35–13/39   Wall to right of Ballycastle descent gully   186
13/37   Odyssey (*photo* K. Higgs)   188
13/40–13/46   The Prow   190
13/51   The Fence   192

14 Ballygalley Head
               Crag diagram   196
14/4–14/13   Ballygalley Head from the Antrim Coast crag   198
14/6–14/10   Castle Gully, left wall   200
14/12–14/13   Castle gully, right wall (*photo* D. Howard)   203

15 The Mourne Mountains
               Area diagram   204
15   Lower Cove   206
15/1   First Corner (*photo* A. McQuoid)   209
15/2   Dot's Delight (*photo* A. McQuoid)   210
15/7   Praxis Direct (*photo* E. Cooper)   212

16 Slieve Beg
16/0   Slieve Beg from the Annalong Valley (*photo* W.
               Annet)   214
16/3–16/6   Main face   216
16/8–16/9   Parallel Lines and Sweetie Mice (*photo* A.
               McQuoid)   219

17 Annalong Buttress
17/1   Thin Crack   222

18 Hare's Castle
18/1–18/4   View from Quarry Platform   224
18/1   Thin Arête (*photo* A. McQuoid)   227

19 Spellack
19/0   View from Trassey path   228
19/2   Mad Dogs (*photo* P. Douglas)   230
19/4   Warhorse (*photo* P. Douglas)   232

	20 Bernagh Slabs	
20/1–20/3	The Slabs from approach track	234
	21. Pigeon Rock Mountain	
21/1	Virgo (*photo* W. Brown-Kerr)	238
21/1–21/4	Left-hand Buttress	240
21/5–21/8	Right-hand Buttress	242
21/5	Class Distinction (*photo* R. Bankhead)	243
21/8	Falcon	245
	22 Eagle Mountain	
22/1–22/6	Crag from approach track	246
22/2	Lassara Grooves (*photo* A. McQuoid)	248

Acknowledgements

Since the crags selected are so widely scattered, it seemed
practically impossible for any one person to compile a balanced
guide. However Calvin Torrans, with his intimate knowledge of
every crag and most routes described, proved to be equal to the
task. In 1981 Calvin, with the groundwork done, left for Canada
and it fell to me to tie this work together. Although the final
selection rested with us, the people listed below freely contributed
their opinions, advice and time.

W. Brown-Kerr, E. Cooper, S. Gallwey, E. Goulding, K. Higgs,
A. McQuoid, M. Manson, A. O'Brien, I. Rea, T. Ryan, C. Sheridan
and D. Somers.

The photographs are the work of many, and are credited in the
list of Illustrations. Those uncredited are by the editors. Our thanks
go to all the photographers for willingly entrusting their negatives
to my chaotic absentmindedness.

Thanks are due also to Emlyn Jones, who has put many hours of
painstaking work into the diagrams, and to Angela Taylor and Jean
Boydell for assistance with photographic and secretarial work.

DAWSON STELFOX

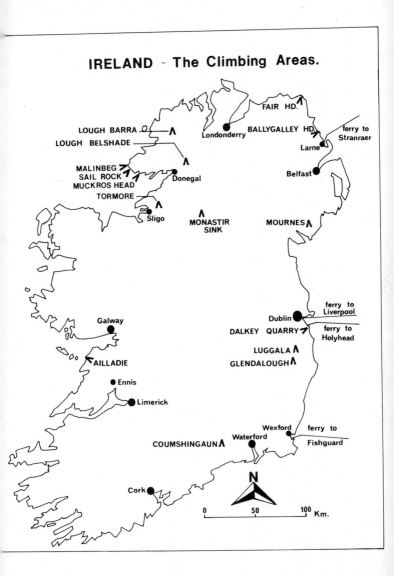

IRELAND - The Climbing Areas.

FAIR HD.
LOUGH BARRA
LOUGH BELSHADE
Londonderry
BALLYGALLEY HD.
ferry to
Stranraer
Larne
MALINBEG
SAIL ROCK
MUCKROS HEAD
TORMORE
Donegal
Belfast
Sligo
MONASTIR
SINK
MOURNES
ferry to
Liverpool
Galway
Dublin
DALKEY QUARRY
ferry to
Holyhead
LUGGALA
GLENDALOUGH
AILLADIE
Ennis
Limerick
Wexford
ferry to
Fishguard
COUMSHINGAUN
Waterford
N
Cork
0   50   100 Km.

Introduction

Rock climbing in Ireland is still in a state of intensive development with many new crags and routes being discovered each year, so it is possible that the best routes have not yet been climbed. Nevertheless, this guide contains more than 300 climbs, all of high quality — some ranking with the best in Britain. The variety is equally good — from short problems in granite quarries and on limestone sea cliffs to 100m of vertical dolerite, and long mountain routes on remote crags. Access is generally easy — only in the Mournes and Donegal are long walks necessary to reach the best routes.

Climbers, and even walkers, are few and consequently queueing is rarely a problem: on the more remote crags, and especially midweek, there is unlikely to be anyone else around. But this attractiveness in turn makes climbing in Ireland slightly more dangerous than in most of Britain. Mountain rescue, especially in the west, is still in its infancy and climbers should be self-sufficient, and prepared for the frequent bad weather.

Ireland's mild climate ensures that rock climbing is possible throughout the year but naturally the high mountain crags are worst affected by wet weather. Fair Head, Dalkey and Clare provide the best opportunities for winter rock climbing. Spring is generally the driest and sunniest season — April and May being the most reliable — with a steady deterioration towards August.

Free climbing has always been emphasised in Ireland and unnecessary aid is discouraged. Chalk has traditionally not been used, and the majority of Irish climbers would prefer to see this tradition maintained.

Notes on using the guide

The crags are described in order, clockwise, starting from Dublin, as Ireland tends to have its crags conveniently situated around the coast. The first three paragraphs of each section, coupled with a map, should give all the facts necessary for finding and climbing on the crag. More detailed information can be gained from the appropriate FMCI (Federation of Mountaineering Clubs of Ireland) guide; these are listed on page 20.

The descriptions follow the standard practice of both Irish, and other Constable, guides.

Numbers on the photographs refer to routes in any particular section. Left and right descriptions are always as found when facing the crag, whether ascending or descending.

With such a wide variety of rock and types of climbing, comparison between grades throughout the country is difficult. In this guide a mix of adjectival grades and technical, numerical grades is given on routes of Severe and above. Below this, the adjectival grade alone suffices. The numerical grade, representing the highest technical difficulty to be found on a given pitch or route, regardless of objective factors, should be universal across the country. The adjectival grade, taking into account such factors as seriousness and remoteness, accommodates the many regional idiosyncrasies. Numerical gradings begin at 3c. A dash (–) indicates where a pitch is below this grade.

Adjectival grades and abbreviations in increasing order of difficulty	*Numerical grades* in increasing order of difficulty, with number and suffix a, b, c.
D Difficult	
VD Very difficult	
	3c
S Severe	4a
	4b
	4a
HS Hard severe	4b
	4c
	4b
VS Very severe	4c
	5a
	4c
HVS Hard very severe	5a
	5b
E1, Extremely severe	5b
E2, (difficulty increasing	5c
etc with number)	6a
	6b

Metric conversion table

Metric measurements are used throughout, but for those not yet
fully conversant with these, a conversion table is given below. The
bold figures in the central columns can be read either as the metric
or the imperial measure. Thus 1 inch = 24.5 millimetres; or 1
millimetre = 0.039 inches.

Inches		Millimetres
0.039	1	25.4
0.079	2	50.8
0.118	3	76.2
0.157	4	101.6
0.197	5	127.0
0.236	6	152.4
0.276	7	177.8
0.315	8	203.2
0.354	9	228.6

Feet		Metres
3.281	1	0.305
6.562	2	0.610
9.843	3	0.914
13.123	4	1.219
16.404	5	1.524
19.685	6	1.829
22.966	7	2.134
26.247	8	2.438
29.528	9	2.743

Yards		Metres
1.094	1	0.914
2.187	2	1.829
3.281	3	2.743
4.374	4	3.658
5.468	5	4.572

Miles		Kilometres
0.621	1	1.609
1.243	2	3.219
1.864	3	4.828
2.486	4	6.437
3.107	5	8.047
3.728	6	9.656
4.350	7	11.265
4.971	8	12.875
5.592	9	14.484

Sq feet		Sq metres
10.764	1	0.093
21.528	2	0.186
32.292	3	0.297
43.056	4	0.372
53.820	5	0.465
64.583	6	0.557
75.347	7	0.650
86.111	8	0.753
96.875	9	0.836

Sq yards		Sq metres
1.196	1	0.836
2.392	2	1.675
3.588	3	2.508
4.784	4	3.345
5.980	5	4.181

A star grading system was not included because precise agreement
on quality, with such a wide variety of climbing, seemed impossible.
Where particular routes are of outstanding quality this is mentioned
in the text, but every route included is well worth doing.

Travelling to, and in, Ireland

The four ports of Larne, Belfast, Dublin, and Rosslare provide easy access to various parts of the country. The Larne/Stranraer and Larne/Cairnryan routes are the most convenient for Antrim and Donegal as well as being the cheapest way of crossing. The Belfast/Liverpool route serves the Mournes, Sligo, and Donegal very easily; entry via Dublin from either Liverpool or Holyhead gives access to Dalkey, Wicklow, and Clare; and the Fishguard/Rosslare route is the most convenient for the Comeragh Mountains or the splendid scrambling and ridge-walking of Co. Kerry.

All the ports are served by main railway lines but a car will be necessary to reach most climbing areas. All sea routes are served by car ferries and, except for a very short stay, it will prove cheaper to bring your own car rather than hire one in Ireland. For the size of its population, Ireland has a tremendous network of roads, and though quality may not always be the best, driving is usually enjoyable and leisurely.

Maps

Although the north is now fairly well served by maps, with a new 1:25,000 issue of the Mournes and 1:50,000 for the rest of the country, the south, with the exception of the Wicklow 1″ sheet, is still covered by the very inaccurate ½″ series, and care must be taken when using these over unknown ground. Maps are obtainable from most bookshops in Belfast and Dublin.

Accommodation

Locations of huts are given in the text, but prior contact with the owner club is necessary:

Wicklow: Dublin University CC, Trinity College, Dublin 2.
              Irish Mountaineering Club, 3 Gortnamona Drive,
              Dublin 18.
Fair Head: Dalriada CC, 43 Cherryfield Avenue, Walkinstown,
              Dublin 12.

Mournes: Irish Mountaineering Club, 32 Russell Park,
                  Gilnahirk, Belfast.
                  Queens University MC, c/o Students Union, Belfast
                  5.
                  Slieveadore MC, 111 Osborne Park, Belfast 9.
                  Glenfoffany CC, 11 Woodland Close, Rushpark,
                  Newtownabbey, Co. Antrim.

Mountain rescue

Although rapidly improving, mountain rescue in Ireland is not a
certainty. Only in the Mournes and Wicklow could help be quickly
on the scene; elsewhere, in the west especially, long delays are to be
expected. Call-outs are initiated by contacting the police (telephone
999) or calling directly to the nearest mountain rescue post. These
are:

N. Donegal:	Strand Road RUC Station, Londonderry.
S. Donegal:	Enniksillen RUC Station.
Tormore: Monastir: }	Enniskillen RUC Station.
Fair Head: Ballygalley Head: }	Ballycastle RUC Station.
Mournes:	Newcastle RUC Station.
Burren:	Gardai — Galway.
Wicklow:	Gardai — Dublin.
	Mountain rescue equipment is kept at Tiglin Adventure Centre, Ashford.

Bibliography

Current FMCI Rock Climbing Guides:

Dalkey, 1979
Wicklow (*Glendalough and Luggala*), 1982
Ailladie – Burren Sea Cliff, 1978
Malinbeg, Muckros Head, and Sail Rock, 1979
Antrim Coast (*Fair Head and Ballygalley Head*), 1981
Mournes, 1980

All information about guides and the Federation of Mountaineering Clubs in Ireland is available from:

Joss Lynam
7 Sorbonne
Ardilea Estate
Dublin 14

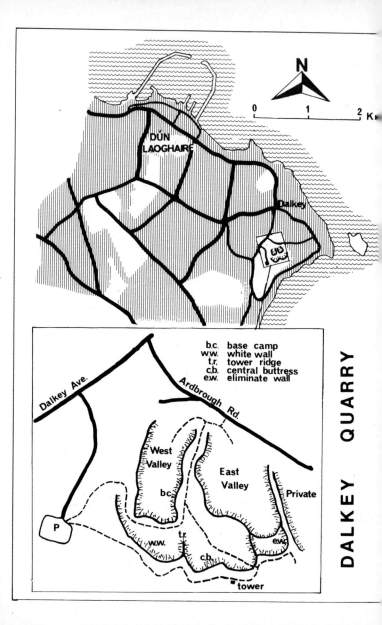

DALKEY QUARRY

DÚN LAOGHAIRE

Dalkey

b.c. base camp
w.w. white wall
t.r. tower ridge
c.b. central buttress
e.w. eliminate wall

Dalkey Ave.

Ardbrough Rd.

West Valley

East Valley

Private

bc

P

w.w. t.r.

c.b.

e.w.

tower

1 Dalkey Quarry, Dublin

GR 2626 Sheet 16, ½″ series

Introduction The Quarry is situated in a fine position on the side of Dalkey Hill. The view extends in a broad sweep across Dublin Bay to Howth, over the city, across to the distant Wicklow Hills and south to Bray Head. Dalkey Hill was the source of granite for the east and west piers of Dun Laoghaire (formerly Kingstown) harbour. Construction continued from 1817 to 1859, the granite being conveyed to the site by the narrow gauge Dalkey Tramway. The East Quarry was known locally as Sevastopol, as it was said that more men were killed there by falls of rock than in the Battle of Sevastopol.

    The importance of Dalkey to Irish climbing is shown by the fact that six guidebooks to it have been produced already. Its proximity to Dublin ensured a fairly steady development since the first routes in the 1940s, as successive generations of climbers used it for midweek training. The Quarry is the property of Dun Laoghaire Borough Corporation and while there have never been any restrictions on the activity of rock climbers, by-laws should be observed. In recent years, fires, litter and, particularly, indiscriminate parking causing congestion on Ardbrugh Road, have led to complaints by local residents.

Access Dalkey may be reached from Dublin by the No 8 bus or by train. From the town Dalkey Avenue runs up towards Killiney Hill, and the Quarry may be reached by taking the second left turn (Ardbrugh Road) or the third, which leads to a car-park just right of the Quarry — see map. The Ardbrugh Road approach is the most convenient for a first visit, since the general layout may be observed from there.

Accommodation Camping is not permitted in the vicinity of the Quarry, and most climbers visit from Dublin or on their way to and from Wicklow.

West Valley

From Ardbrugh Road the West Valley is entered at its northern
end. The first small crag on the left is Practice Buttress and provides
some pleasant bouldering. Keep to the path through the barrier of
brambles, and on the left the cliff becomes steeper and higher. The
first prominent buttress rises steeply for about 15m and is marked in
the middle by light patches of rock. Pilaster takes a line up the face
of this narrow buttress.

1/1 Pilaster

15m VS (4c) Maguire, Kopczynski, 1951
Start: Up the small slab below some light patches of rock. Move
strenuously right to gain a ledge at 5m. Go left up the ledge towards
the edge of the buttress. Reach a higher ledge and move delicately
right until it is possible to gain a good ledge and belay at the top. It
is probably easier to move up slightly right from the first ledge at
5m.

1/2 Bushmills

12m HVS (5b) McHugh, 1970
Start: In the recessed part of the cliff to the right of Pilaster in a
vertical corner. Climb the initial crack with difficulty to a sloping
ledge. Up over the bulges on top on good holds.

1/3 Bracket Wall

18m VS (4c) Winder, O'Sullivan, 1949
Start: 4m right of Bushmills and left of a large brown undercut
block. Move up on small holds to base of drill hole. Pull up and
stand on quartz bracket (crux) and move slightly right. Cross a
smooth slab.

1/4 Charleston

15m HS (4a) McCormack, Stephenson, 1958
Start: Corner just right of Bracket Wall just left of the brown block.
Climb a corner for 4m to the overhang. Move out left to the nose
(crux) and then straight up to top.

West Valley of Dalkey Quarry. View from the top of the Upper Cliffs
looking towards Dublin

1/5 Mahjongg

12m HVS (5a) Young and party, 1973
Start: Near the bottom left-hand end of the central slabs at a point where a thin crack starts from an overlap and runs up to the cliff top. Climb the overlap and gain the crack. Follow this past ledges to the top.

1/6 Levitation

15m S (4a) Kenny, Morrison, 1950
Start: To the right of Mahjongg below the left-hand end of the central slabs at a point where a crack, starting about 6m above the ground, runs up from right to left. The slab to the left of the crack is marked by brown patches where flakes have fallen away. Up easy rock to the bottom of the crack. Delicately gain the crack and follow it to the top.

1/7 Paradise Lost

16m VD Calvert, Perrott, 1950
Start: Just right of Levitation, below central slabs about 4m left of an ash tree. Move up on to a small ledge and climb a thin crack at the right-hand end to another ledge. Climb wide crack to gain the top of the prominent flake. Step delicately right and continue up diagonally for about 2.5m, then back left and up by a delicate move to gain a ledge. Scramble to top.

1/8 Scavenger/Exertion

18m HVS (4c, 5a) Moloney, O'Flynn, 1962; Windrim, 1973
Start: From Base Camp — the traditional meeting place and gear dump. The slab above is referred to as Yellow Slab.
1   **9m** Scramble diagonally left to reach the overhanging corner and crack. Step down and around corner to foot of crack. This is Exertion.
2   **9m** Climb overhanging crack, good finishing holds.

West Valley, Dalkey Quarry. B.C. marks Base Camp and E.G. the descent route of Easy Gully

1/9 D Route

24m S (3c)

Start: Just left of Base Camp. Climb diagonally left over large blocks. Gain a ledge at 4m just to the left of the Yellow Slab and move up to large flake. Continue straight up, gain an outward-sloping slab and from this make a difficult move on to a similar slab above. Move left up the slab to block (possible belay — common to D, E and F Routes). Descend the short slab and climb the groove above its lower edge. Gain a good ledge and exit via the vertical drill hole.

1/10 E Route

24m VS (4c)

Start: At Base Camp.

1   16m Surmount the steep rock using the scimitar flake and drill hole at 1.5m to gain the Yellow Slab above (this can be avoided by following the initial ramp on F Route until the slab is reached). Continue up for a metre and then traverse diagonally left to the corner of the overhangs. Move slightly down at the corner to an outward-sloping slab (D Route). By a difficult move gain the slab above. Belay on blocks. (This point is common to D and E Routes.)

2   8m Descend the slab for a few feet and climb the groove above. Gain a good ledge, and finish from here as for D Route at overall grade HS; or move to the right end of the ledge and climb the downward-sloping steps with poor finger holds to the top — delicate and exposed.

1/11 F Route

18m HS (4b)

Start: A few feet right of Base Camp by two small ash trees. Climb the narrow ramp with a large flake on its right for about 4m. From the end of the ramp move up a corner for 1m and then out right to a narrow ledge. Gain a ledge above and move right to a possible belay. Move up left to a ledge just right of a projecting block, the bottom of which forms a prominent overhang as seen from below. Swing out left and up on to this block to a ledge. Climb the wall above at its right-hand edge. (The final pull up after the swing out

may be avoided by traversing left and back right above to the top.
This reduces the whole standard to S.)

1/12 Gargoyle Groove
15m HVS (5b) O'Leary, Harmey, 1957
Start: Below the final slab just before the start of Easy Gully
(ascent/descent scramble). Up this short easy slab to base of groove.
By strenuous moves gain the ledge at 9m. Continue up past the
gorse bush and go right below the overhang. Surmount this at its
easiest point.

To the right of Easy Gully is a steep clean slab containing the
following routes:

1/13 Winder's Slab
11m HS (4b) Winder, 1952
Start: At bottom left corner of slab. Up diagonally right on small
holds until they fade out. Long reach to small hold. Use this to move
up and exit by block.

1/14 Winder's Crack
11m VD Winder, 1949
Climb the crack in middle of slab to top.

1/15 Paul's Edge
12m HVS (5a) Hill, 1953
Start: Right-hand end of slab. Gain slab and move up and right to
edge with difficulty. Continue up past bore hole. Sustained climbing
to top.

The remaining West Valley routes are situated at the north-west
end of the valley opposite Pilaster.

1/16 Jameson Ten
14m VS (4b) Dick, 1966
Start: Under a small overhang at the left-hand side of a smooth
vertical wall. Climb to a detached flake under the friable overhang.
Surmount the overhang and follow the right-hand of the two
shallow grooves until a step across to the left at the peg. Continue
up groove. Mantelshelf to finish.

1/17 Calypso
14m S (4a) Ryan, Butler, 1976
Start: Climb the slab and traverse right to large ledge. Step left and
up wall to top.

1/18 Tramp
9m VS (4c) Ryan, Higgs, Latham, 1976
Start: First obvious corner right of Calypso. Ascend to ledge at foot
of corner. Up corner and crack with difficult exit.

1/19 Shuffle
9m HVS (5b) Windrim, 1976
Route takes the prominent arête left of Dirty Dick. *Start*: As for
Dirty Dick. From the bottom of the corner move up and out left on
to arête. Climb arête, moving across leftwards.

1/20 Dirty Dick
9m VS (4c) Ryan, Higgs, Latham, 1976
Start: Take the slanting corner right of Tramp. Climb the corner
with difficult exit.

Gargoyle Groove

Jameson Ten. Willie Brown-Kerr on the moves into the right-hand
crack (p. 32)

Central Buttress on the Upper Cliffs. D marks the descent stair from the
Upper Cliff Path to the Plateau; b = belay positions (p. 33)

The Upper Cliffs

From the Ardbrugh Road entrance the Upper Cliffs are reached by
following the grassy ridge which divides the East and West Valleys.
The main features of the Upper Cliffs, from left to right, are:

A   Central Buttress — the prominent mass of rock on the right
      below the old signal station
B   Tower Ridge — the obvious ridge of rock
C   White Wall — the steep area of rock forming the extreme
      right of plateau

1/21 Central Buttress

29m E1 (5b, 4b, 4b) Maguire, Morrison, Kenny, 1951
Start: Scramble up to large ledges below main buttress from left.
1   **11m** Climb the small nose at the left-hand end of ledges right
of a small niche (crux) up and left (peg). Climb the corner and
traverse left to a belay ledge (peg).
2   **9m** Climb the corner using the hanging block and traverse left
to good belay (pegs).
3   **9m** Move left and up into a small overhanging V-corner. Gain
the slab above and follow this to top.

1/22 Thrust

*24m HVS (5a) Jones, Duggan (Pitch 1), 1968; Ryan, Windrim
(Pitch 2), 1976*
Start: Immediately below the steep corner, left of Preamble.
1   **12m** Climb the wall to the foot of the steep corner. Ascend this
to the large flake. Poor belay on spike to the right.
2   **12m** Direct Finish: from the large flake continue up a thin
crack to a large ledge. Traverse left under the bulging head wall,
pull on to a ledge. Avoid loose rock on left by climbing diagonally
rightward to a tree belay.

Upper Cliffs. The skyline arête is that of Tower Ridge, with the climber
at the top of Pitch 2: b = belay positions

1/23 Preamble

23m VS (4c) O'Flynn, Moloney, 1962

Protection poor.

Start: Right of Thrust and below the top pitch of Giant's Staircase. The route follows an ill-defined rib from just above the ground level to the start of Pitch 2 of Giant's Staircase.

1   15m Climb up to the left of the rib for 3m and step right across the rib. Continue up to gain the ledge.

2   8m Climb the corner above (Pitch 2 of Giant's Staircase) and finish up Tower Ridge.

1/24 Giant's Staircase

26m S (3c)

Loose rock changes the start to the second pitch.

Start: Below the great overhang on the east flank of Tower Ridge.

1   18m Climb up left over a series of square-cut ledges with vertical drill holes. Difficulty increases with height — peg at crux. Belay on the ledge to the left of the overhang and below the corner.

2   8m Climb the corner above, treating the rock with respect. Difficulty eases towards the top. Finish up Tower Ridge.

1/25 Graham Crackers

20m HVS (5a) Richardson and party, 1977

Start: 20m to the right of Giant's Staircase. Climb the wall for 3m to an awkward mantelshelf. Move up left to a series of ledges. Climb the face on good holds to the bore hole. Continue up the wall by a hard move to gain the nose. Move right on a series of ledges to gain a horizontal crack. Move left and up a wall to a ledge. Continue on to Tower Ridge.

Giant's Staircase, Calvin Torrans on Pitch 1

1/26 After Midnight

18m E2 (5c) Windrim, Latham, 1977

Start: As for Graham Crackers. The route takes the vertical overlap right of Graham Crackers. Climb the wall to ledge. Move upwards and then left to a horizontal bore hole. At the base of the pillar gain height to mantelshelf on to a jug. Peg runner in place. Climb to a flat edge and mantelshelf on to the ledge. Swing out right to a nut belay on the slab on Pitch 2 of Tower Ridge.

1/27 Tower Ridge

40m D

The continuous prominent ridge that comes out from the cliff at a point just left of the radio beacon on top of the hill.

Start: Immediately right of the steep nose of the ridge.

1   14m Climb up the groove right of the ridge to a block belay.

2   9m Traverse out to the left across a rock ledge and pull up on to a slab on the ridge. Continue up over a steep step to a block belay. Alternatively, climb straight up on to the ridge above the first belay.

3   9m Move up on to the narrow exposed section; continue to a small notch level with the right-hand slope. Belay.

4   8m Scramble up easy rocks to the top.

1/28 Helios

34m HS (4b/c) Kenny, Kopczynski, 1951

A superb long steep climb, adequate protection can be arranged.

Start: Below the slightly overhanging section at the bottom of White Wall. An outward-sloping ledge (the Catwalk) crosses the wall about 2m above ground level.

1   18m Gain the Catwalk at its right-hand end and traverse left into the corner with a vertical drill hole. (Possible to climb directly to this point from below.) Pull up and swing up left to reach a small ledge left and above the drill hole. Move up right in a corner and then left on to an edge. Move up the edge for 1m before moving on

Graham Crackers, Tommy Curtis moving up the steep wall above the nose

to a ledge on the right-hand wall. Move up into the groove above.
Peg belay.

2   8m Climb the groove to a nick on the left edge. Either
continue straight up or make a long step across the groove to a ledge
on the right. Move left under a little triangular nose and up to stance
with block belay. Pitches 1 and 2 are usually taken as a single pitch.

3   8m From the block gain a slab out on the right and follow this
to the top.

1/29 In Absentia

*29m VS (5a) Kopczysnki, Ohrtman (simultaneous solo ascents),
1952*

A beautiful route. The peg on the final wall greatly reduces the
seriousness of this climb.

Start: At the base of White Wall just right below a little sycamore
tree in a nook, 4m. Step up on a block, then up on to a little rib on
the right. Cross left and up by a hard move to reach the sycamore
tree ledge. Continue above to a ledge, move left towards a
triangular nose with a drill hole running along the bottom. Continue
left and move around the nose to a niche on the far side. Move up
on to the bridge of the nose and ascend the wall above (peg in place)
to the top. Ash tree belay.

1/30 Hyperion

21m HS (4c) Kenny, Maguire, Morrison, 1951

A magnificent route on perfect rock.

Start: At the base of White Wall, below and to the right of a little
sycamore tree at 4m.

1   9m Climb the 4m slab moving slightly right to a small ledge.
Continue up into a corner and by way of a crack gain the top at a
prominent block. (Alternative start can be made by following the
thin crack to the right of the slab to the right-hand top of the
prominent block.) Step up from this and cross leftwards on to the
slab. Peg belay.

White Wall on the Upper Cliffs of Dalkey Quarry, with Willie
Brown-Kerr on Helios

2   12m Move left and climb the corner on the right of a long projecting block (or pass under the block and climb up on its left) to a niche. Peg runner. Move left by a long delicate step round on to the face. Climb the steep wall above to ash tree belay at the ledge. Scramble to the top.

East Valley

The gate on Ardbrugh Road leads on to the East Valley section of the Quarry. To the right, a wide gorse and grass-covered ridge, The Band, leads by an easy walk to the Upper Cliffs plateau. The flank of this ridge gives a number of routes up to 20m on generally sound rock. On the opposite side of the valley the Ivy Chimney area has become very popular and taken some of the pressure off the Eliminates, at the extreme end on the left, where the white slabby floor of the Quarry rises up towards the boundary wall.

The routes on the left side of the valley start some 12m right of the cottage garden on Ardbrugh Road, beginning with a section of more broken and vegetated rock. Beyond this is a smooth wall followed by steeper broken rock, then slabs and finally Eliminate Wall.

1/31 Erewhon
9m E1 (5c) Latham, 1976
Sustained in difficulty with visionary protection.
Start: Below and right of a line of bore holes, on the smooth wall. Climb the wall via the bore holes to the top. Crux is leaving the second bore hole.

1/32 Street Fighter
12m VS (4c) Higgs, Young, 1976
The upper section gives good wall-crack climbing.
Start: Just to the right of Erewhon, some 4m left of The Shield. Ascend steep broken rock to a good ledge at 5m. Move left to a narrow sloping ledge and climb the thin crack in the wall above.

East side of the East Valley, Dalkey Quarry. E.W. marks Eliminate Wall

E.W.

«1/32
33

1/33 The Shield
15m E2 (6a) Windrim, 1978
Start: As for Street Fighter. Ascend steep broken rock to a good ledge. Continue up the rightward-trending crack, difficulty increasing with height.

1/34 Eliminate A
15m VD 1950
Good slab and wall climbing.
Start: At the bottom left corner of Eliminate Wall. Climb the corner of the slab for 8m to the corner of the wall. Up the steep section on good holds. Move left to the edge and continue to the top. Drill hole thread belay.

1/35 Eliminate A Dash
17m S (4a) Winder, 1950
A good technical climb.
Start: From the bottom left corner of the lower slab, other approaches possible. Follow a straight line from the bottom corner of the slab to a slight bulge in the wall about 9m above and about 2m right of the left edge of the wall. Surmount the bulge and move up right. Reach up on the right and gain the ledge. Climb the short wall above.

1/36 Eliminate B Dash
14m VD Kenny, 1950
A highly recommended route.
Start: Left of a hawthorn bush at the base of the wall and under a small sloping shelf about 3m up the slab. Gain the shelf and move up over the flake. Continue up until it is possible to traverse left to a crack. Reach around on the left and gain the ledge. Climb the short wall above to the top. Instead of traversing left the route may be followed directly to the top.

Left of the more broken rocks which flank the grassy ridge leading to the Upper Cliffs plateau, there is an area of smooth steep wall and right of this again there is a wide area of smooth slabs.

1/37 The Ghost

23m E2 (5c) Windrim, Windrim, 1976
Start: At flakes 5m left of wall and slabs junction. Ascend
diagonally leftwards along crack to niche. Alternatively step up on
to slab and traverse on small holds (harder). From niche climb
diagonally rightwards and then straight to top.

1/38 Stereo Tentacles

14m HVS (5a) Young, O' Murchu, 1973
A very good route with two sections of sustained climbing
connected in its natural line by a teaser move.
Start: Below a recess left of the obvious orange section of rock.
Continue up the smooth slab on the left to a ledge. Up to the
recessed slab, peg runner, and climb this, continuing left to the top.
Spike belay.

2 Glendalough, Wicklow
GR 095965 Sheet 16, $\frac{1}{2}$" Series/Wicklow 1"

Introduction Glendalough ('the glen of the two lakes') lies on the
east side of the Wicklow Mountains. It is an impressive glaciated
valley popular with hill walkers, and the ninth-century monastic
ruins have added to its attraction for tourists.

The main cliff (Camaderry) is located on the north side of the
valley just beyond the upper lake. It is a granite cliff and the best
climbing is on the area known as Twin Buttress, at the west end.
The predominant type of climbing on this cliff is open-face climbing
with finger cracks. Protection is reasonable and there are some old
pegs *in situ*.

Access Glendalough is about 50 km from Dublin and may be
reached by taking the T7 past Bray to Kilmaconogue, then the T61
through Roundwood to Laragh and the L107A to the car-park in
the valley. There is a bus service from St Stephen's Green in Dublin
twice a day — St Kevin's Bus Co, Roundwood, telephone 818119.

To reach Twin Buttress continue past the ruined buildings and
along the track leading to the head of the glen, on the right of the
Glenealo stream. Leave the zigzags where the track turns left for
the second time and follow up a well-defined foot trail. This leads to
the foot of Acorn Buttress, the conventional base camp. This
approach takes about 40 minutes from the car-park.

Descent
1 The cliff may be descended by a broad heathery rib to the west of
   the cliff.
2 Above the slab route Expectancy at the west end of the top of
   Twin Buttress there is an abseil hook. From the foot of the slab a
   track may be followed to base camp.
3 The descent at the east side to Twin Buttress is the most
   commonly used, but the start is hard to find and the descent can
   be very slippy in wet weather. Go east from the top of the main
   central waterfall for 50m and down a slightly heathery depression
   towards the edge of the cliff (about 20m). The small track then

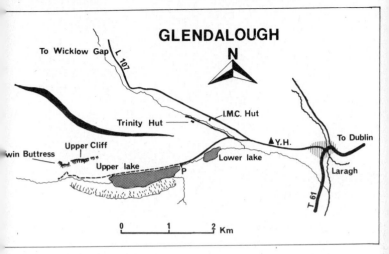

runs east down a 2m rock step and continues eastwards to reach the slope running down to base camp.

Accommodation Camping is prohibited in the area and the nearest site is in Roundwood. There is a youth hostel in Laragh and numerous houses provide bed and breakfast accommodation. There are two climbing huts in the area (see map), for the use of which it is necessary to contact the club secretaries.

2/1 Cracks on the Garden of Eden
39m VS (4b) Morrison, Gorevan, Lynam, Perrott, 1951
Follow the shallow gully which flanks the western wing of Twin Buttress passing the base of a prominent slab (Expectancy) on the right. Continue to a narrow south-facing wall which is split by two well-defined cracks. This route takes these cracks.
Start: Below the short corner.
1   **12m** Up corner and follow a wide crack up rightwards to belay in trees.

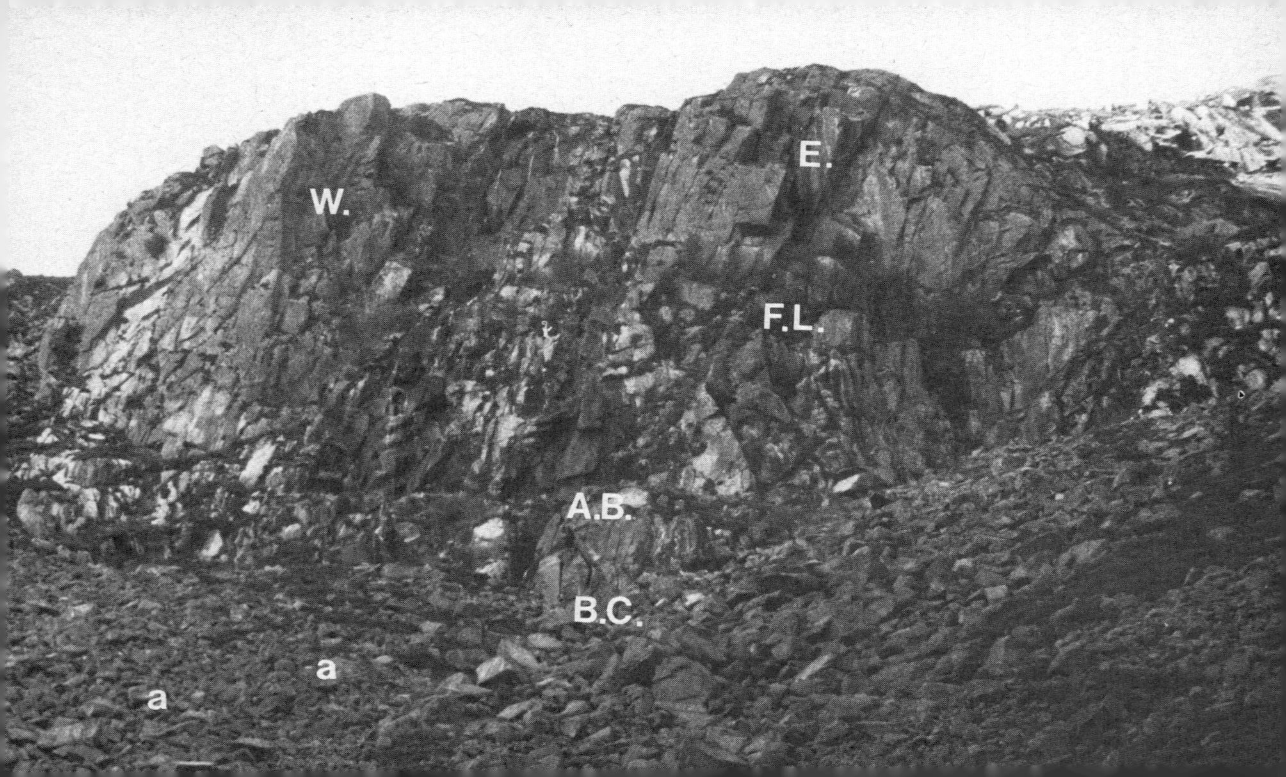
W.
E.
F.L.
A.B.
B.C.
a
a

2   13m Traverse left to base of steep crack. Climb this to a
horizontal break, continue up second part of crack and belay on
ledge below steep groove.
3   14m Climb groove passing a rocking block, continue up steep
crack, exiting left near top.

2/2 Expectancy
21m VD Maguire, Kopczynski, Rothery, 1954
This very popular climb takes the best line up the clean slab to the
right of the last route.
Start: Below a cracked groove near the centre of the slab. Climb
groove; at 7m move slightly left and continue to top using cracks
and large holds.
     The normal means of descent from the top of the cliff is by
abseiling down the Expectancy slab; there is an abseil hook in place.

Main face of West Wing of Twin Buttress

2/3 Quartz Gully
54m HS (3c,4b,3c) Kenny, Winder, 1954
Start: At the base of the west wing of Twin Buttress, and somewhat
to the left of centre, a white quartz vein runs up the face. The route
follows this line.
1   24m Climb the short corner for 3m and up to a grass ledge at
the base of the quartz vein. Move right and climb the wall on good
holds to ledge. Block belay.
2   21m Step up left on to a block and climb vein to a spike.
Traverse left along sloping ledge and climb a rightward-trending
crack (crux) back to the quartz vein. Continue up the groove to
ledge on the right.
3   9m Climb the crack and short corner to the top.

Twin Buttress of Glendalough from the valley path. The line a-a marks
the easiest approach to Base Camp (B.C.). Just above this is Acorn
Buttress (A.B.) with the West (W) and East (E) Wings of Twin Buttress
behind. F.L. marks Forest Ledge and the Upper Cliffs lie above and to
the right

2/4 Holly Tree Shunt

55m VD Kenny, Maguire, Winder, 1950

Start: The route takes the obvious gully and corner just right of the quartz vein.

1   **24m** Climb the first pitch of Quartz Gully.

2   **13m** From the ledge continue up the gully to a large recess. Belay.

3   **18m** Climb the arête on right; step left into gully, move up and climb the corner on good bridging holds. Continue on top.

2/5 Prelude/Nightmare

74m VS (4b,4b,4a,4c) Kenny, Winder, Ohrtmann, 1953

Start: From the heather ledge near the lowest part of the main face, just right of a small cave.

1   **14m** Just right of the cave climb a short wall on small holds to gain a sloping ramp. Move left along ramp and climb the wall above; continue up vegetated corner to large ledge.

2   **20m** Climb the slab above and step out left around the overlap, move left to crack and follow this to ledge (awkward). Pull over a bulge and climb up to stance and flake belay.

3   **16m** Traverse left into a corner; up this and continue up until possible to traverse right across the face to a small ledge (Nightmare ledge) at the base of a short vertical crack. Nut belay.

4   **24m** Nightmare pitch: climb the crack and traverse right across small slab to a holly tree. Climb the groove above, moving right on to the arête near the top.

2/6 Spillikin/Fanfare/Speirbhean

83m HVS (4c,5a,4c) Kenny, Winder, Hill, Rothery (Pitch 1), 1954; Winder, Kenny (Pitch 2); 1953; Rothery, McCall (Pitch 3), 1956

This superb combination takes in most of the best climbing on the main face, and is high in the grade.

Start: At the right-hand end of heather terrace at the base of a quartzy groove.

Cracks on the Garden of Eden and Expectancy: a marks the position of the abseil hook

1   43m Climb groove and move right to a stance on top of a pillar. Climb slightly vegetated crack on left and continue up until possible to attain thin crack in wall. Climb this to a small ledge on right. Thin moves above lead to a good belay ledge.

2   20m From ledge make a delicate move left on to arête. Move up delicately to a ledge (the groove above is Scimitar HVS, 5a). Traverse left and follow slanting line up face to a small ledge (Nightmare ledge) below thin steep crack.

3   20m Step down and traverse left to base of a groove near the arête. Gain groove and up to a small ledge; move up wall above and then traverse left to gain arête (delicate and exposed). Follow arête to top.

2/7 Spillikin Ridge
86m E2 (4c,5c) Kenny, Winder, Hill, Rothery, 1954; Goulding (after Spillikin fell), 1967; Torrans, Darby (first free ascent), 1981
Start: At the right-hand end of the heather terrace below a quartzy groove.

1   43m As for Pitch 1 of the Spillikin/Fanfare/Speirbhean combination.

2   43m Climb groove directly above belay for 3m until possible to traverse right into a vertical crack. Climb crack with difficulty (past protection peg) to small overhang. Climb the overhang and sharp crack to another overhang. Traverse left under this to a groove (resting place). Move up and follow a rightward-trending groove to a small exposed stance near the arête. Climb the arête above with difficulty, then continue more easily to the top.

2/8 Sarcophagus
84m HVS (4b,5a,5a,5a) Goulding, Ingram, 1961
The classic route for the grade, with a magnificent corner on Pitch 3.
Start: As for Spillikin Ridge.

1   24m Climb Spillikin Ridge but instead of moving left at 20m traverse right and climb parallel cracks, stepping right to gain stance at the bottom of a corner.

West Wing of Twin Buttress

2   12m Move up the corner and climb a steep section direct to a large ledge and tree belay below the big corner groove.
3   32m Move up and start the corner with difficulty; continue up more easily until the corner steepens (large spike on left), then gain holds on the arête on right. Climb the short crack and move rightwards into corner; up this to a stance in a niche. Nut belay.
4   16m Climb the groove above to a tree and continue up the awkward corner crack to the top.

East Wing of Twin Buttress

This is the somewhat broken and forested buttress to the right of the waterfalls.

Acorn Buttress forms a separate small outcrop (15m high) at the foot of the east wing of Twin Buttress, directly above base camp. Owing to its proximity to base camp, it has become very popular. The routes here range from VD to VS but it is just about possible to wander about any way on the buttress. However, Acorn Crack, S, follows the wide crack on the left and has several variation finishes; Provo, VS, takes a central line finishing up thin parallel cracks; and over on the right side Facilis Decensus, HS, starts up the groove at the lowest point of the buttress and continues more or less directly up with an arête finish.

   The next two routes, Bruces Corner and Celia, start around the left edge of Forest Wall, while Aisling Arête and Lethe start from a prominent belay block on Forest Ledge and follow obvious crack lines up Forest Wall on either side of the block. After finishing one of these routes it is recommended that you abseil back to Forest Ledge to start the next.

Quartz Gully, Robert Bankhead on the crux moves of Pitch 2

2/9 Bruces Corner

21m VS (4c) Rodgers, McDermott, 1969

Start: Either by scrambling along the ramp below and to the left of Celia (often wet) to a grass ledge below the obvious corner, or abseil to the base of the corner. Climb the delicate corner groove to a small overhang. Move out right around this and continue up the corner to the top.

2/10 Celia

29m VS (4b) Goulding, Gaffney, Higgins, 1963

Start: From the belay block on Forest Ledge.

1   16m Move left and climb around the left-hand end of Forest Wall, and up a heathery ramp to a steep wall with two cracks. Belay below the right-hand crack.

2   13m Climb the right-hand crack; near the top move out right to the arête and up this to stance and belay. Finish as for Aisling Arête.

2/11 Aisling Arête

28m VS (4b,4a) Kenny, Moss, 1953

This route takes the wide crack at the left edge of Forest Wall. Can be done in one pitch.

Start: Just to the left of the belay block on Forest Ledge and immediately left of the crack.

1   16m Climb the left edge of Forest Wall and then step right into the wide crack; continue up the crack to a good ledge.

2   12m Climb the short corner above and gain arête on right. Follow this and scramble up past a perched boulder to belay.

The skyline arête of Spillikin Ridge with the obvious clean corner of Sarcophagus to the right

2/12 Lethe
29m VS (4c) Kenny, Winder, Rothery, 1954
Start: Below a crack to the right of the belay block on Forest Ledge.
Climb the slightly rightward-trending crack to a ledge. Awkward
step right into crack and up this with difficulty to base of short
corner groove. Instead of climbing the short groove above (Lethe
Direct, HVS 5a) move leftwards into a groove; up this and finish up
arête to belay.

2/13 Forest Rhapsody
110m S or VS (4c,4a,3c,4a,4a) Rothery, Winder, 1952
A popular route; only the first pitch is VS, and this can be avoided.
Start: From the grassy shelf above Acorn Buttress, mid-way
between the waterfall and the trees.
1 12m Start below a sharp arête. Climb the arête which becomes
delicate at 5m and continues so until the top; *or* scramble up a
grassy rake to the back of the arête.
2 20m From the top of the arête step up and traverse left
(awkward), then move up to a quartz groove. Follow this to a stance
and block belay.
3 26m Step right and move up past trees to a blocky corner; up
this and then follow an easy scramble leftwards to a block belay at
the foot of Forest Wall.
4 30m Gain the sloping ledge on the right; at the right-hand end
of this make a delicate step up and move around corner. Climb a
short groove to the obvious crack; follow the crack to a large ledge
and belay.
5 22m Move slightly right and ascend by a series of
mantelshelves; continue up a corner on the left, then gain a ledge on
the right; finally step back into the groove and escape left.

Sarcophagus, Dermot Somers on Pitch 3

2/14 Ifreann Direct and Chimney
35m E1 (5a,5b) Goulding, Tobin, Rothery, Kavanagh (Pitch 1),
1966; Winder, Masterson, McCormack (Pitch 2), 1953
This fine combination takes a line up the right side of Forest Wall
and starts at the base of a clean steep finger crack, directly below
the right-hand edge of a prominent overhang. The start is best
reached by following Forest Rhapsody to the scrambling path in the
trees (Pitch 3). This brings the climber directly to the base of the
crack.

1   20m Climb the sustained finger crack to the overhang.
Continue up the crack on the right and follow the slabby rock to a
holly tree.

2   15m Move slightly right and up into the overhanging
V-chimney. Climb this with increasing difficulty to ledge at the top.
This pitch is often damp and an alternative is to climb the short
square-cut chimney above and slightly to the left of the holly tree —
Ruth's Chimney (4a). Gain the top of the crag via the top pitch of
Forest Rhapsody.

The next three routes are located in the **Upper Cliffs** which lie to
the right (east) of the eastern wing of Twin Buttress.

2/15 Silent Movie
90m E3 (5c,5c) Dean, Stronach, 1981
Start: 13m left of Cornish Rhapsody at the lowest point of the slab
and beneath a small overhang at 7m.

1   43m Climb up under the overhang, then right and up to a
pedestal. Make a rising traverse left above the overhang (5c) and
round the arête to a ledge. Climb the crack in the arête for 9m, then
delicately ascend on the slab, moving first right, then left and back
right again to gain a faint white break rising rightwards to a peg
belay under the great roof.

East Wing of Twin Buttress: F.L. marks Forest Ledge

11 12 13 14 F.L. 2/13

2   22m Step right on to a steep slab below a break in the overhang (small wires). Climb this and the corner above for 6m to a small spike. Make a rising traverse to the left (poor small wires) for 6m to reach a good handhold beyond the edge. Step down round the edge to climb a good layback behind a large inverted flake. Belay in the cracked slab above on the right.

To finish, either climb to the ledge visible on the arête above right, then up a clean cracked slab (22m) or descend by abseil from the top of the inverted flake.

2/16 Cornish Rhapsody
110m HVS (4c,5b,-,-,-) Stephenson, Deacon, 1959
Start: At the bottom of the obvious quartz vein on the big slab.
1   36m Climb the quartz vein until a groove leads left to a small ledge beneath the overhang. Traverse right and up to a grass ledge and block belay (delicate and poorly protected pitch).
2   20m Crux pitch: step off the block and climb the wall above. Move delicately right then back left to gain a narrow diagonal ramp (often damp). Follow the ramp right and belay in a scoop.
3   18m Climb slab to the right and move around corner; continue up past patches of gorse to a wide crack. Belay.
4   21m Traverse left for 6m and up by crack to holly tree below the overhang. Belay.
5   15m Move up through the holly and climb the overhang to a crack above which is followed to the top.

The Upper Cliffs of Glendalough

2/17 Cuchulainn Groove

45m HS (4a/4b) Kenny, Winder (alternate leads), 1950

This route takes the most obvious corner groove in the Upper Cliffs and is located some 80m right of Cornish Rhapsody. The groove is usually damp.

Start: By scrambling to the base of the groove from the right.

1   **15m** Climb the groove to good ledge at 15m. Belay.

2   **30m** Climb the groove to a steep section, pass this on good holds and continue up crack to a large grass ledge. Tree belay. Either abseil off (preferred) or continue up and rightwards to the top.

Aisling Arête, Eddie Cooper on the initial crack from Forest Ledge

3 Luggala, Wicklow
GR 155078 Sheet 16, ½" Series/Wicklow 1"

Introduction. Luggala is a granite cliff above the north-west corner of Lough Tay. The nearest village is Roundwood. Steep overlapping granite slabs with poor protection are what one chiefly encounters, but the crag provides excellent climbing in very impressive and picturesque surroundings.

   The crag consists of Creag Conaisearach — a steep wall high up on the left; the central main face, separated from Creag Fasra below by a large grassy terrace; and Creag Thuaidh, to the right beyond a gully bounding the main face — North Gully.

Access To reach Luggala, take the T7 from Dublin past Bray to Kilmacanogue, then the T61 past the Sugarloaf Mountain, and the L161 at a right turn signposted for Sally Gap. Continue up this road until you reach the gates of Luggala Estate. This point can also be reached from the north via the Sally Gap from Blessington and Tallaght or Enniskerry. The estate is private property and cars must be parked at the gates, from which the cliffs can be seen. Follow the road down to the first house. Leave the road and follow a track down the field towards the lake. At the corner of the fence head down to where the river leaves the lake and cross it by stepping stones. A track leads from here to the boulder field.

Descent
1 From Creag Conaisearach descend by South Gully.
2 From Creag Fasra descend by Terrace Corner to South Gully.
3 From Creag Thuaidh descend by North Gully.
4 From the main face descend by 1 or 3.

Accommodation There is a camp site in Roundwood, and the climbing huts of Glendalough are within easy reach by car.

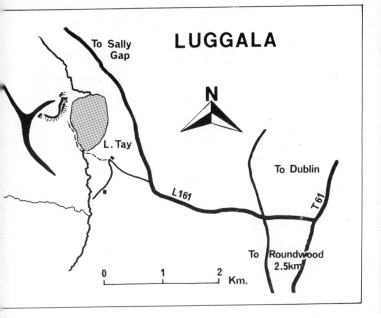

Creag Conaisearach

About 50m up the main descent gully (South Gully) above Terrace
Corner there is a large horizontal ledge at the base of a steep wall.
The first three routes start off this ledge.

3/1 Hyrax

54m HVS (4b,4c) Higgs, Young, 1975

Start: In a small recess beneath two holly trees at the far left-hand
end of the ledge; above and left of a detached block.

1   27m Climb the steep recess (easiest on the left) and move up
past the holly trees to a short corner crack. Up corner to blocky
ledge and continue up a leftward-trending slab to an overlap and
jammed spike. Step around left below overlap and up a ramp to
ledge and tree belay.

2   27m From the tree ascend diagonally rightwards to a narrow sloping ledge below a green wall. Climb steeply to a horizontal flake (runner) and traverse rightwards across the wall to the arête. Make a difficult step up and continue up steep rock on good holds to the ledge. (Possible belay.) Climb the short slab above to a large ledge and belay.

It is preferable to escape to the main gully by scrambling down leftwards to a path.

3/2 Caravan
50m E2 (5b,5b/c) Higgs, Windrim, Windrim, 1976

This impressive route takes the obvious line through the overhangs in the centre of the wall.

Start: Near the right-hand edge of the large horizontal ledge, above large trees and below a recessed crack.

1   25m Climb crack for 5m and pull out left at overlap. Move leftwards to ledge; climb up steeply, moving diagonally left beneath the overhang to reach a small foot ledge in the centre of the wall (protection peg in place). From the left end of ledge climb up and through the obvious gap in the overhang. Move up diagonally right and across delicately to a shallow groove; follow this to a long ledge and tree belay on right.

2   25m Move back left along ledge 5m to a groove. Up this until possible to traverse diagonally right to a stance (possible belay) below an overhung corner. The crux: move up corner and gain good hold just below lip of overhang, pull up to layaway holds on the left edge and gain the V-groove above quickly. Step right on to ramp and continue up easily to nut belay on ledge.

Luggala from the lakeside. S.G. marks South Gully; C.C., Creag Conaisearach; C.F., Creag Fasra; M.F. main face; C.T., Creag Thuaid; and C., Conifer Terrace: d marks descent routes from the upper and lower paths

3/3 All Along the Watchtower

62m VS (4b,4a,4b) Higgs, Windrim (alternate leads), 1976
Start: At the right end of the horizontal ledge directly above two large trees. The route starts up a short rightward-trending corner to reach the large white platform.

1   32m Belay in a crack on the left. Gain the top of the large white platform on right by awkward moves up the corner. Leave the ledge out to the left via the narrow ramp; up this until possible to climb up on to small ledge. Make a delicate move left to a wide crack; up this and continue to tree (belay here if preferred). With aid from tree climb the steep wall above to good stance (peg and nuts).

2   15m Make a descending traverse rightwards, down slab and across blocks (exposed). Continue traversing right on better holds to gain stance on lake side of arête. Nut belay.

3   15m Climb the clean groove above, moving left to arête at the bulge. Continue up groove to ledge and nut belay.

3/4 Curved Air

80m VS (4a,4b,4b) Windrim, Higgs (alternate leads), 1976
Start: About 40m along terrace from Terrace Corner, at the undercut base of a clean leftward-trending groove.

1   20m Pull up small ledges on right and move left into the groove, passing an awkward bulge at 5m. Follow the groove to a clean white ledge. Nut and small thread belay.

2   20m Climb the crack on the left and gain the slab with difficulty. Move along a vegetated ramp to a short bulging wall, climb this on large flake holds and continue easily to middle of undercut wall. Peg belay *in situ*.

3   40m Climb the overlap on the right and immediately traverse back leftwards to gain steep crack in centre of wall. Climb the crack and leftward-trending groove above (awkward moves near the top) until a narrow ramp leads to a ledge. Nut belay. Easy ground to the top.

Creag Fasra, Luggala

Creag Fasra

3/5 Stepenwolf
70m E1 (5b,5b,4a) Higgs, Windrim, Ewen, 1977
The route takes an almost direct line up the wall left of Muskrat Ramble.
Start: About 12m left of Muskrat Ramble below a leftward-trending undercut slab.
1   25m Pull on to slab and up this for 4m to a small spike on the right wall; using this gain a good foot ledge. Move up slightly left and climb a difficult bulge on small holds. Continue up the narrow leftward-trending ramp (awkward to start) to a good stance and tree belay.
2   25m Move up short slab on left to the obvious groove in wall. Pull up using sharp flake crack, step across right and climb wall on good holds to a hanging block. Delicate balance moves above block to gain sloping ledge (crux). Climb overhang above on large flake holds and follow short groove to a narrow slab on left. Up this to belay at cracked blocks.
3   20m Climb cracked blocks to heather ledge. Step up right and climb cracked slab to nut belay at back of Terrace.

3/6 Muskrat Ramble
80m HVS (4b,5a,4c) McKenzie, Blake, 1975
A superb intricate climb.
Start: Approximately 90m below Terrace Corner, at the base of a lichenous slab, and a few metres to the right of a very steep wall.
1   32m Climb slab diagonally left to a small spike runner at 9m. Climb up to short corner and move up and gain groove above. Up this to grassy ledge and traverse left to tree belay.
2   25m Climb steep corner behind tree (crux) to gain good holds near top; using these pull on to ledge (protection peg). Climb the steep rightward-trending ramp, one awkward move to start. At top of ramp move up and slightly leftwards to gain a short groove. Up this to a small holly tree and stance at the crevasse.

Main face, Luggala

3   23m Move horizontally left for 4m to bulging wall, and make a
strenuous mantelshelf on to the ledge above (well protected).
Traverse delicately rightwards to a crack and climb this to gain the
arête on the left edge of the slab. Follow this to the Terrace.

   Variation to the final pitch (VS, 4b): After the mantelshelf
continue traversing rightwards to the base of a large corner crack
(Psycho Direct finish). Peg belay *in situ*. Climb the corner crack to
the Terrace, difficult near the top.

3/7 Silent Spring
45m HVS (5a,4a) Latham, Ryan, 1976
Start: Approximately 50m to the right of Muskrat Ramble is an
embayment with a prominent gully line (Intermediate Gully). Right
of this gully is a steep buttress with a large, leftward-trending
heather ramp on its lower part. The climb starts halfway up this
ramp below some green rock.

1   35m Climb up and right and gain top of a 3m slab. Pull on to a
large leftward-trending slab. Climb this, mainly on the left ledge to a
protection peg. Step around left into base of main groove and up
this to a small rectangular overhang. Climb this on the left (crux) to
a small ledge. Continue up short corner groove and pull on to
sloping ledge above.

2   10m Climb steep rock on right to grassy ledges. Up these and
exit a muddy corner to the Terrace.

3/8 Pine Tree Buttress
92m S (3c,3c,3c,4a,3c) Lynam, Crean, 1949
The classic S on the crag.
Start: To the right of Silent Spring is a very prominent slabby
buttress. Start just right of a boundary wall and below a small slab
4m right of a hanging holly tree.

1   12m Climb the slab and move left to the foot of a chimney
between a steep slab and a detached flake. Up this (awkward) to a
ledge. Belay.

Muskrat Ramble, Clare Sheridan on the first pitch

2   **18m** Go around the corner on the left into a V-scoop and up this to a wide crack on the left. Climb the crack and continue up an easier-angled crack to a holly tree. Belay.

3   **9m** Step right and gain crest of buttress by climbing through small holly trees. Scramble up vegetation to big flake lying on side.

4   **40m** Crux pitch — climb the subsidiary slab on the left edge of the buttress (exposed and hard to start). After a few metres move on to the main slab, via a flake crack, where the climbing becomes easier. Continue up slab to foot of a wall. Go right on to a bulge and climb up to a large heather ledge. For a belay scramble 10m up vegetation and easy slabs to a small recess. Nut belay.

5   **13m** From the recess climb up diagonally left past a large flake (often damp). Move left and climb up into a scoop below an overlap. Climb overlap using a crack at the right side and exit on to the Terrace about 10m below and to the left of the Pine Tree.

Variation, VD: If last pitch is wet, continue traversing left across the scoop at belay level below the overhang and climb left of overhang up vegetated slabs to the Terrace.

Main face

3/9 Clingon/Claidheamh Solais
50m VS (4a,4c,4b) Rice, Redmond (Pitch 2), 1971; Hand, McKenzie 1971 (Pitch 3)
Start: As for Spearhead.

1   **13m** Climb the first pitch of Spearhead.

2   **20m** A fine pitch. From the belay move up to the left and climb the overlap (crux) moving diagonally right to gain a stance. Climb the obvious groove above which is delicate near the top. Gain a superb belay ledge on the right. Nut belay.

3   **17m** Step back right and follow a flaky crack up to the roof. Make long step left and move up until an exposed traverse right can be made to a groove. Up this to the top. Block belay.

Pine Tree Buttress, Willie Brown-Kerr on the initial moves of Pitch 4

3/10 Spearhead

60m HVS (4a,4b,4a,5a) Deacon, Stephenson, Winder, 1955
A fine route which is mainly HS except for last pitch which is just HVS.
Start: At the extreme right-hand end of Conifer Terrace directly below the big roof. Belay in a short cracked corner.
1   13m Scramble up easy slabs on the left, then up a flake crack on the right and follow leftward-sloping slab to a small stance at a cracked block. Nut belay.
2   21m From the belay make a long step right to small grass ledge. Descend slightly rightwards and then move up to the main diagonal fault. Follow this to a short steep corner. Nut belay.
3   8m Climb the corner and traverse right to a stance in the corner under the roof of overhang. Peg and nut belay.
4   18m Crux: hand traverse out right until possible to swing around arête on to a slab. An awkward step up and then easily up slabs to belay at a wedged block.

3/11 The Gannets

60m E2 (5c,5a) Rice, Redmond (aid point), 1971
An exposed route with reasonable protection. Superb route finding.
Start: At the extreme right-hand end of the Terrace. Belay in the cracked corner as for Spearhead.
1   25m Move out right and climb a slab to a thin crack, climb up and rightwards to the base of a square-cut corner. (Peg *in situ*.) Using peg for aid (handhold) climb corner and move around the nose to gain a steep groove. Up this to good holds in horizontal crack. Pull up and gain a small foot ledge out on the arête. Step right and climb the groove (crux) to a large grassy ledge on right. Nut and chockstone belay.
2   35m Climb the detached block on the right and step off this to gain a slabby groove on left. Move up slab to slightly overhanging corner. Climb this and pull on to slab on right. Continue easily up slabs to belay (nuts).

Spearhead, Dermot Somers on the crux hand traverse of Pitch 4

Creag Thuaidh

3/12 Dance of the Tumblers
55m HVS (5b,5a) Richardson, Young, Harris, Mulhall, 1972
Start: One-third of the way up North Gully, some 4m right of a cave
and below an obvious leftward-trending gangway up the edge of the
gully wall.
1   30m Move up on to the gangway and climb the curving green
slab to reach a short corner. Step up and move around left to a
resting place, pull up to a small ledge beneath an overlap. Crux:
climb overlap moving left to large spike hold on arête; using this,
gain the sloping stance above. (Possible belay, pegs needed.) Make
a slightly descending traverse rightwards below the overhang
(delicate and exposed) until a step down leads to better footholds.
Continue traversing right to gain a grassy ledge. Peg belay.
(Alternatively after the traverse climb up on to a slab and nut belay
in a flake crack.)
2   25m Ascend diagonally left for 3m and pull up a short wall;
continue up on good layaway holds to a groove on the right. Follow
this to reach a sloping ledge below an overhanging niche/chimney.
Exit this with difficulty to gain a spectacular position and a large
spike hold high on the left. Continue more easily to the ledge.

Dance of the Tumblers, Dermot Somers on the crux moves up the
arête

4 Coumshingaun, Comeragh Mts, Waterford
GR 3211 Sheet 22, ½" Series

Introduction Coumshingaun is perhaps the finest example of a glacial corrie in the British Isles, the walls of which provide good quality climbing in a superb situation, and are, for the most part, made up of a friendly, knobbly conglomerate.

The corrie has three main cliffs, facing south, east and north respectively. The south-facing cliff is easy-angled and sunny, with some pleasant slab climbing. The east-facing cliff, the main back cliff, is the largest of the three — about 350m in height and over 500m long. The difficulties are confined to the initial 200m, above which it is possible to traverse off. The cliff is divided into two tiers of rock by a ledge at 100m and the best rock climbs to date are located on the steeper upper tier, as the lower one is seldom in condition because of water seepage. The north-facing cliff is the steepest of the three, and a strongly developed vertical jointing provides strenuous climbing up steep jamming cracks.

Access The corrie is best approached from the Carrick-on-Suir to Dungarvan road (T56). Park directly below the coum beside a bridge with an unsignposted side road leading off to the east. The coum should not be mistaken for a similar, though smaller and dry, coum directly to the south. From a gate beside the bridge a path leads across the stream, up a field and, via the right-hand side of the coum, to the lake. About 45 minutes from the road.

Accommodation Camping, either by the road or the lake, is probably the most convenient option.

North-facing cliff
This cliff should be approached via a high path above the southern shore of the lake. Descent is best accomplished by continuing up the mountain until a sheep track is encountered and then traversing off to the left to a wide gully, which leads down to the eastern end of the cliff.

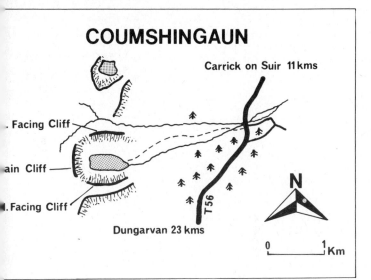

4/1 Emperor's Nose

50m E1 (5b,5b) Gallwey, Lee, 1980

This climb takes the steep corner on the left side of the arête with
the prominently overhanging nose near the top. The arête is located
on the left-hand side of the gully at the eastern end of the cliff (not
the wide descent gully).

Start: Traverse in to the bottom of the corner from the gully on the
right. Start just left of a square-cut overhang at 5m.

1   **27m** Climb the corner until the crack in the back of it closes at
approximately 15m. With difficulty reach a large hold on the arête
to the right. Swing out on to this and mantelshelf on to it. Continue
up the arête to a ledge. Step back left into corner and up easy
ground to a flake belay.

2   **33m** Climb the overhanging fist-jam crack past the nose to exit
on to a ledge on the right just below the top.

4/2 Dark Angel
60m HVS (4c,5a) Jacob, Gallwey, 1980
Right of the arête of Emperor's Nose is a gully forming an obvious
corner in its upper section. This route takes a ramp line on the left
(eastern) wall of this gully.
Start: In a sentry box overlooking the lake, just around the corner
from the gully.
1   30m Climb the crack to a grassy ledge. Traverse left for 3m
and climb the flakes to a ledge below the prominent roof. Move
right into the main corner and belay.
2   30m Climb the corner to the top. Crux is surmounting the first
overlap.
    An alternative (5b) start to Dark Angel takes the obvious
jamming crack that splits the east wall of the gully, to join the route
after 12m at a large ledge.

4/3 Crooked Smile
60m VS (4b,4b) Gallwey, Hernstadt, 1981
This climb takes the twisted chimney/corner system that splits the
arête formed between the main face of the cliff and the left wall of
the large gully at the western end of the cliff.
Start: At the base of the arête on a large ledge. Traverse in from the
right.
1   20m Climb the obvious flakes. Step out on to the right-hand
wall and traverse right to a crack splitting a detached block. Climb
crack to top of block and step across to a large ledge. Belay in a
corner.
2   40m Climb the corner and traverse left to the base of the
overhanging chimney. Climb chimney to gain hanging slab leading
up left (crux). Climb the slab until forced out left on to the arête by
the overhang. Climb straight up to the top of the crag.

    A crack high on the left-hand wall of the deep gully to the right of
Crooked Smile is taken by Birdman, E1 (5b). The lower pitches are
fairly scrappy, with a strenuous overhang at mid-height.

North-facing cliff of Coumshingaun from the lakeside. Only Emperor's
Nose is visible

East-facing (Back) cliff

The following climbs are located on the upper tier. This is best approached by continuing past the base of the north-facing cliff to a stream in the south-west corner of the coum. After gaining some height it is possible to traverse out on to the main face via the halfway ledge. Descent is best achieved by traversing off left from the top, along sheep tracks, until the stream is reached once more. The easiest ground is found about 50m past the stream.

Owing to the size of this cliff, it is recommended that plenty of time be allowed for completion of a climb and the descent. A torch may prove useful.

4/4 Jabberwock
95m HVS (5a,4b,4b) Gallwey, Jacob, 1982

Takes the faint corner with an overhang at 35m, 4m to the left of Gargantua.

Start: At the base of an undercut slab.

1   40m Pull up strenuously on to the slab and continue up to a short overhanging corner. Climb this with difficulty to a stance immediately above. From here a high runner may be placed on the left. From the stance traverse diagonally rightwards (two marginal Rock runners) to gain the arête where it steepens. Traverse back into the centre of the slab to the overlap for a good Friend runner. Continue up the centre of the slab to the overhang. Climb this on large holds to belay on a stance above.

2   40m Traverse diagonally leftwards to a break on the arête. Climb the arête on good, though fragile, holds to gain a grassy ledge. Climb directly up face using a good crack to gain another grassy ledge with a willow tree. Belay.

3   15m Climb directly up slab to the right of the tree (poor protection) to gain the terrace and belay well back.

Care is needed over arrangement of protection, with many small Rocks being recommended.

Dark Angel, Stephen Gallwey on the direct start

4/5 Gargantua

90m HVS (5a,4c) Gallwey, Jacob, Hernstadt, 1981

This climb takes the chimney/corner that splits the arête, just left of the southern main face gully.

Start: At the base of a steep corner which becomes a flared chimney higher up. There is a wet seepage spot on the ledge and a detached boulder to the right.

1 **45m** Climb the corner strenuously to gain the bottom of the chimney. Ascend chimney with increased difficulty as the left wall fades out (crux). Pull out of top of chimney into a corner and ascend this more easily to a sloping ledge to belay.

2 **45m** Continue up corner to a triangular grassy recess. Up left-hand side to grassy ledge and climb short corner above. Trend right across broken ground to good rock belay.

A further 20m of scrambling reaches a large terrace, traversed by the sheep tracks.

4/6 Colossus

104m VS (4c,4c,4c) Gallwey, Hernstadt, 1981

This climb takes the right-hand side of an enormous triangular flake resting on the halfway ledge, immediately to the right of the Southern Main Face Gully. The right-hand side of the flake is vertical and forms an obvious corner.

Start: The base of the corner is best approached by traversing in from the left along the halfway ledge, encountering a 6m crux section at the Southern Main Face Gully.

1 **35m** Climb the corner between the flake and the main face. The crack goes off-width in its upper part, though it may be bridged all the way. Protection may be had at the resting points and by a brief sortie left beneath the overhang on the left wall. Belay on top of flake.

2 **24m** Traverse diagonally leftwards and climb a thin crack going straight up the face to the base of an undercut corner and belay.

East-facing cliff of Coumshingaun from the lakeside: d indicates the descent route towards South Gully

3 **45m**+ Climb corner to overhang. Move left on to the arête and gain a small ledge above. Climb a vegetated corner to broken ground (possible belay on doubtful rock). Trend rightwards up on to the grassy terrace and belay well back. A doubled rope, with one end pulled through by the leader is useful to get a good belay.

All the above routes suffer from fairly vegetated upper sections, although the initial pitches are superb. This, combined with difficult approaches and descents, makes these climbs serious mountaineering routes in all but perfect conditions. A long spell of dry weather is recommended before you attempt climbing in the corrie, as the surrounding vegetation greatly increases difficulties.

Jabberwock, Stephen Gallwey on the first ascent

AILLADIE

Road L 54

Way Down · Genesis · Long Ledge Wall · Rockfall · Gallows Pole · Aran Wall · Box of Chocks · Mirror Wall

Dancing Ledges · High Tide Line

Lisdoonvarna →

Road L 54 · wall · Gt. Balls of Fire

Mirror Wall

AILLADIE · Ennistymon · Lisdoonvarna · L 54 · Black Head

ENNIS · T11 · To Galway · To Limerick · T 1

N

0 · 10 Km

5 Ailladie, Clare
GR 009004 Sheet 14, $\frac{1}{2}$" Series

Introduction Ailladie is an 800m long limestone sea cliff with routes varying in height from 8m to 30m. It lies out of sight below the Lisdoonvarna/Ballyvaughan road (L54), 11 km north of Lisdoonvarna and about $1\frac{1}{2}$ km beyond where this road reaches the coast. The climber encounters steep rock with sharp incut holds and a rough texture reminiscent of gritstone. Most routes take crack lines, and protection is reasonable.

Access Descent is either by abseil where indicated in the route descriptions; or at the extreme left-hand (northern) end of the crag, at its lowest point; or by Descent (D), the second and broken southward-facing corner at this end. The routes are described looking from left to right, from the seaward side. The steep smooth wall, right of Descent, is Long Ledge Wall, characterised by a long narrow ledge 3m from the ground at its left-hand end.

Accommodation Off-season accommodation is easily obtainable in Lisdoonvarna. Climbers have hitherto camped by the roadside. Water can be obtained from a small spring at one of the laybys above the crag — difficult to find.

5/1 Ground Control
16m VS (4c) Ryan, Windrim, Higgs, 1976
Start: This route takes the obvious leftward-trending cracks which cross the centre of Long Ledge Wall. Climb a thin crack to the Long Ledge at 3m. Ascend diagonally leftwards up the cracks to the top.

5/2 Atomic Rooster
16m HVS (5b) Windrim, Windrim, 1976
Start: Near the right end of Long Ledge Wall there is an obvious overhanging and curving groove: start under this, 10m left of Genesis. Pull up into the groove and climb this to a small ledge on the left at 7m (crux). Ascend the groove on the left of a rib. Step right on to the rib and follow a steep crack to the top.

5/3 Genesis
16m HS (4b) Mullhall, Young, 1972
Start: This route is at the right-hand end of Long Ledge Wall, in an obvious corner, the upper part of which forms a conspicuous leftward-trending slabby groove. Gain a ledge at the bottom of the corner. Ascend steeply past some rocking blocks (crux) to the upper slab. Climb the crack and slab above to the top.

5/4 Bonnain Bui
15m VS (4c) Mulhall, McKenzie, 1972
Start: This route takes the obvious groove which starts at mid-height, under an arête 5m right of Genesis. Climb broken rock on the left side of the arête to a flake at mid-height. Surmount this (crux) to enter the groove. Up this to top.

5/5 Nutrocker
15m HVS (5a) Young, Mulhall, 1972
Start: On a boulder below the steep corner crack 8m right of Genesis. Climb easily to where the corner steepens and so up to a mid-way ledge (crux). Continue more easily up the corner.

Right of the rock fall there is a 28m high steep and smooth wall: Aran Wall. The most obvious feature near the left end of Aran Wall is a pair of rightward-trending parallel cracks.

5/6 Rollerball
28m E2 (5c) Windrim, Ryan, Higgs, 1977
Start: At the top of the rock fall there is a short pleasant corner with a small overhang at the start (Blasket, S). A few metres right of this, on Aran Wall, there is a steep corner which starts at mid-height. This route takes the corner, which is reached from the right by a line of weakness. Start below a yellow stain on the rock just to the left of, and below, the obvious pair of parallel cracks. Climb the wall to a hard move at 4m and gain a niche. Move up and diagonally left to reach a resting foothold on the slab below the corner. Ascend the slab and up the overhanging corner to the top.

Long Ledge Wall, Ailladie

5/7 Gallows Pole
28m E2 (5c) Higgins, Ryan, Windrim, 1977
Start: Directly below the pair of rightward-trending parallel cracks at the left end of Aran Wall. Climb steeply up a groove to a small overhang and gain the base of the parallel cracks. Climb the cracks (crux) directly to the top— sustained and strenuous.

5/8 The Marchanded Crack
28m E1 (5b) Richardson, Levy, 1975
The easiest route on Aran Wall and very worthwhile.
Start: On boulders just to the right of Gallows Pole. Trending rightwards, climb steeply up the wall to a sloping ledge. Gain another sloping ledge on the right. Move up left into a small niche and then up to a larger niche (crux). Move right and up to gain large holds which lead spectacularly to the top.

5/9 Skywalker
32m E2 (5c) Murphy, Ryan, 1981
Start: As for Moments of Inertia, taking the crack immediately to its left. From the ledge at the bottom of the corner move left and up to the crack. Follow this to the huge hanging block (crux at large jutting flake). Finish up the wall above at the right-hand end of the block.

5/10 Moments of Inertia
30m E3 (6a) Colton, Somers, 1977
Right of the cave near the right of Aran Wall there are two very large blocks projecting from the face.
Start: On boulders under the right-hand projecting block. Traverse left under the block to gain the base of the corner forming the left side of the block. Up the corner, and gain a good hold halfway along a yellow streak on the right (crux). Using this, climb the arête and corner above to a large ledge on top of the block. From the left end of the ledge climb a crack to the top.

5/11 Box of Chocks
24m S (3c) Mulhall, Douglas, Leonard, Flynn, 1972
Start: Right of Aran Wall there is an obvious overhanging groove —
Line of Fire, E2 (5b). The first corner right of this is a double corner
with two grooves. Ladda, VS, takes the left-hand groove and this
excellent route takes the right-hand groove. Climb the corner crack
(crux near the bottom) to the top.

5/12 Promised Land
24m E1 (5b) Colton, Somers, 1977
Start: On boulders below a system of steep cracks, 8m left of the
final corner on the Dancing Ledges. Trend leftwards up the crack to
a resting niche. Continue steeply up to a small overhang and exit
right on to a ledge. Belay here or continue to the top. Sustained and
strenuous.

Mirror Wall
This is the very impressive 30m-high wall south of the Dancing
Ledges, with three large corners at its southern end. Access is by the
Dancing Ledges, involving scrambling over boulders at low tide in
calm weather, or by abseil at Pis Fluich. The starts of these routes
are all affected by the sea and so care with the tides is essential.

5/13 The Ramp
*45m E1 (5b,5a/4c) Somers, Dwyer 1977; Torrans, Sheridan (first
free ascent), 1977*
This is probably the best climb on the cliff. Near the right end of
Mirror Wall there is a very obvious rightward-trending stepped
ramp.
Start: On a boulder at the base of this.
1   28m Step across on to a ledge directly under the base of the
ramp, and mantelshelf on to a second ledge 3m higher. Climb the
groove above to where the left wall becomes overhanging and move
out to the right (crux). Up the ramp to where it steepens and hand
traverse right. Step down on to a good ledge and peg belay. The peg
may well be badly corroded and need replacement.

Ground Control. The climber is Dermot Somers

2 17m Climb up to a small ledge and traverse right until it is possible to climb to the top.

5/4 Pis Fluich
30m HVS (5a) McKenzie, Mulhall, 1972
Another excellent route with impressive climbing at a reasonable standard.
Start: On boulders under the third and steepest corner right of Mirror Wall. Climb down from the boulders and step into the corner. Ascend on very rough rock until the corner steepens. Climb the thin crack to resting footholds at mid-height. Continue up to a good ledge. Easier climbing to the top.

Around the arête south of Pis Fluich is the steep smooth **Stone Wall**. South of this again is the impressive inset cliff of **Falla Uaigneach**. Further south is **Boulder Wall** — a complex area of cliffs with two boulders on the top. The first obvious feature of Boulder Wall is a white slab with a ledge running along the bottom under it.

5/15 Doolin Rouge
25m HVS (5a) Blackburn, Holliday, 1979
Start: Takes the left-hand side of the slab left of Great Balls of Fire. Abseil down to the left end of the ledge. Climb about 1m right of the arête to a large ledge. Trend left to a small overhang on the arête. Over this, and up to a small ledge on the arête, and up right to top.

5/16 Great Balls of Fire
26m HVS (5a) Walker, Buschel, 1977
Start: Abseil down to the ledge and belay below the wide crack at its right-hand end. Climb the crack to where it ends at a small overhang. Trend up leftwards and traverse delicately left using two horizontal cracks. Climb a good crack more easily to the top.

Rollerball, Sean Windrim on the first ascent

5/17 Black Magic
26m HVS (5a) Irving, Wynne, 1977
A serious route — very little protection for 15m.
Start: 2m right of Great Balls of Fire. From the end of the ledge enter a groove and gain a small ledge. Climb the black corner to another ledge. Move delicately right to a narrow ledge and climb the steep wall for 5m to a horizontal crack. Move rightwards for 2m and climb a thin crack to the top.

5/18 Salt Rope
24m E1 (5b) Irvine, Wayne (one aid point), 1977: Murphy, Maun (first free ascent), 1981
Start: About 10m right of Great Balls of Fire there is an obvious corner. Salt Rope follows an obvious thin crack 3m left of the corner. Abseil down to a small tidal ledge at the bottom of the corner. Climb the corner for about 5m to where the crack starts and the corner veers to the right. Follow the crack to the left and then straight up (sustained interest) to rejoin the corner at the top. Finish up this. Excellent protection.

Gallows Pole, Ken Higgs on the first ascent (p. 102)

Mirror Wall and The Ramp (p. 103)

The Ramp, Dermot Somers on the first ascent, first pitch

6 Monastir Sink, Fermanagh
GR 119336 Sheet 26, 1:50,000

Introduction The Fermanagh/Cavan area abounds in little-developed
limestone and gritstone crags, of which Monastir is perhaps the
most prominent. This is a limestone cliff giving excellent steep
climbing with abundant finger pockets. It dries quickly and is very
sheltered — so much so that carnivorous midges are often a problem
in summer.

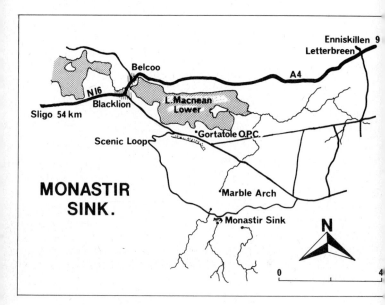

Monastir, left wall. The climber is on the initial moves of Mike's Route,
with Spider starting below the cave immediately to the right

Access The crag is situated on the Marlbank Scenic Loop,
south-east of Blacklion/Belcoo. The loop is signposted from the
Blacklion–Florencecourt road, and approximately halfway round
the loop (6½ km) there is a small layby at the top of the crag. Reach
the foot by descending a small path on the right of the layby,
looking south. Climbs finish on the road. The cliff is at the end of
the blank valley at the bottom of this path, with a stream sinking at
the base.

Accommodation With prior application it may be possible to camp
in the grounds of, or stay at, Gortatole Outdoor Education Centre,
Florencecourt. A new routes book is kept here for the area.
Camping is possible with permission of local farmers.

The crag is split into two walls of rock, the stream sinking at the
foot of the right wall.

6/1 Mike's Route
20m VS (4b) Rodgers, Orr, 1966
Start: In the corner to the right of the huge flake at the foot of the
Left Wall. Surmount the overhang and gain the stump. Continue up
to the top of the pinnacle. Move out right on to the wall and climb to
the tree.

6/2 Spider
20m HVS (5a) Rodgers, 1967
Start: Below the cave 2m right of Mike's Route. Gain the cave by a
thin move. Traverse right to a sapling and up left to a good ledge.
Move up and right to below the small overhang. Semi-layback to
gain horizontal crack, and traverse right with difficulty to the arête.
Up this to finish.

Monastir Direct: c marks the cave belay position

6/3 Monastir Direct

33m HVS (5a) McDermott, Cousting (one aid point), 1967; Cowan, Wray (first free ascent), 1975

Start: The obvious corner rising from the river bed.

1   14m Bridge up the cave mouth to gain the crack. Strenuous climbing leads to a ledge on the left. Good thread belay just inside the cave (for those with night vision the cave provides an interesting escape!).

2   19m Follow the wide crack above by bridging to the top of the flake (sparse protection). Continue up the crack above. Belays a long way back.

6/4 Black Bastard

27m VS (4b) Cole, Smith, 1980

Start: 20m right of Monastir Direct up the river bank, below a cave. Traverse left and up into the cave. Move out left of cave and surmount overhang moving right. Climb the obvious corner above.

7 Tormore Crag, Sligo
GR 735442 Sheet 7, $\frac{1}{2}''$ Series

Introduction The crag is situated on the north side of Glencar Valley and comprises a two-tier buttress high above the western end of Glencar Lake. The crag is 15m to 30m in height, is composed of reef limestone, and gives steep climbing. The rock is compact and has a rough texture offering excellent friction and abundant finger pockets.

Access Take the Manorhamilton road from Sligo (T17) for about 8 km, then follow the scenic route around Glencar Lake to the old crushing mill at the north-west end. Cars can be parked opposite the mill. Follow an indefinite path just to the left of the overhead mine cable which runs from the lakeside to the top of Tormore. After approximately 30 minutes' walk a wide grassy ramp leads rightwards to the left edge of the upper tier crag. The routes described are all on this tier.

Accommodation There is a small camping area on the lake shore opposite the mill, and off-season accommodation in Sligo.

The approach path up the grassy ramp leads to the base of a large flake crack. The first route starts here.

7/1 Ferdia
24m HVS (5b) Higgs, Ryan, 1977
Start: Route takes the flake crack, moves left around the overhang and into the clean-cut corner. Climb flake crack to ledge below overhang at 12m. Step up delicately and move left around overhang to corner crack. Climb past jammed blocks to resting place below clean-cut overhanging corner. Move up corner a few feet to gain small sharp finger holds on the right wall. Using these, traverse across wall to arête (crux) and up this to small stance. Step up and move left, finishing with care. Metal stake belay well back.

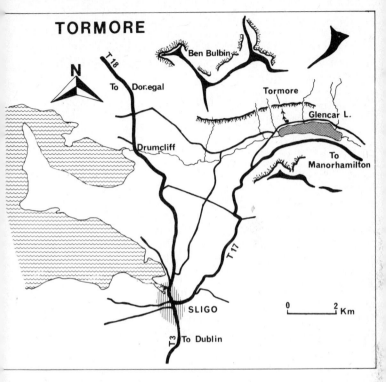

7/2 Above the Salt

27m E2 (5c) Torrans, Sheridan, 1977

Start: 5m right of Ferdia below the prominent white scar which is situated near the top of the crag. Climb short shallow groove to horizontal crack, move up and left on pockets to reach deep jug. Traverse left on jugs to short corner (hard to enter). Up corner to ledge on left. From the large rocking block traverse right, with feet level with bottom of block. Make a wide bridge to reach jugs and

Tormore Crag, left-hand wall. D marks descent route

continue up wall on pockets to a thin crack on right side of the white scar (scoop). Move left and climb into scoop with difficulty. Small jug and sidepull to reach crack and jammed blocks. Crux: climb crack to reach flat holds and poor jam. Keep left near top. Stake belay.

To the right of Above the Salt there is a steep clean wall with a flattened bush at half-height. Just to the right of the bush a steep crack runs the complete length of the wall. The next route takes this crack.

7/3 Warthog
24m HVS (5b) Higgs, Ryan, 1977
Start: 2m left of a triangular-shaped, 3m-high pinnacle leaning against the wall. Climb the strenuous crack until possible to bridge on to flake on the left wall. Continue steeply to good holds at the horizontal break at 12m. Small rest ledge on right. Step back left and climb crack, passing an awkward protruding block; continue more easily to top of crack. Traverse diagonally right to grassy ramp and top. Stake belay.

7/4 Halfbreed
24m HVS (5a) Ryan, Higgs, 1977
Start: At base of the crack which forms the left-hand side of the triangular pinnacle. Climb the crack to the top of the pinnacle. Move up the steep crack on the left (crux) to reach sidepulls further left. Continue up, trending leftwards to a stance. Climb up rightwards to a good ledge below a bulging wall. Traverse left to the protruding block on Warthog. Finish up Warthog to top.

7/5 Strongbow
24m VS (4c) Ryan, Higgs, 1977
Start: At the base of the crack which forms the right-hand side of the triangular pinnacle. Climb the crack to the top of the pinnacle. Trend rightwards up a crack to a spacious ledge. Climb the short wall above until possible to move leftwards on to a blocky ledge.

Climb the bulging wall to reach hidden jugs on the slab above
(crux). Continue more easily to the top.

The right-hand side of the flattened-bush wall is flanked by an
obvious corner. The next route takes this corner.

7/6 Condor
24m HVS (5a) Ryan, Higgs, 1977
Start: This route takes the obvious corner opposite the left end of a
crevasse that splits the ground about 10m out from the foot of the
cliff. Climb the corner easily until it becomes square-cut and vertical
at mid-height. Using finger jams, surmount this section (crux) to
good holds. Trend leftwards avoiding loose rock to the top.

Right of Condor there is a bulging buttress which falls into a
depression. The next route starts at the right-hand side of this
depression at the 2m-high flake leaning against the face.

7/7 Weekend Warrior
30m E1 (5c) Torrans, Sheridan, 1980
Start: At the detached flake, at bottom of a crack that runs to the
top of the crag. Climb up over flake to thin crack. Up crack to
overhanging groove and crack. Climb the groove (crux) with good
flake on right. Continue up crack to the top.

7/8 Leda
27m E1 (5b) Torrans, Sheridan, 1977
Start: At base of crack formed by the left side of the flake. Climb
blocky crack to reach deep crack behind flake. Continue up crack to
small sloping ledge on left. Keeping this ledge at shoulder level,
traverse left for 2m to good ledge and crack. Climb crack to reach
good jug on right. A series of jugs lead up right to a bulging wall;
from the foot of wall move up and left to narrow ramp (crux). Use a
sloping hold to reach deep crack at back of ramp. Finish slightly left
to top. Stake belay.

7/9 Fergus
21m S (4a) Sheridan, Torrans, 1977
Start: About 1m right of Leda. Route takes the obvious corner with
the cracked right wall. Climb easily up left to vegetated ledge.
Continue past small holly tree and climb corner on good bridging
holds and using cracks on right-hand wall to reach bulge near top.
Climb bulge and continue up easier ground to top.

   Some 10m right of Fergus there is Landmark Boulder, a 9m-high
boulder with a sharply cracked surface. The next batch of routes
start in the vicinity of this boulder.

7/10 Sparrow
27m HVS (5a) Torrans, Sheridan, 1977
About 1m left of Landmark Boulder there are two prominent
diagonal cracks trending from right to left. This route takes the
lower diagonal crack.
Start: At base of flaky crack left of Landmark Boulder. Climb crack
to huge flake at start of diagonal crack. Climb diagonal crack, using
good jugs on lip of crack, to yellow stain on steep wall (resting
place). Up wall on jugs and move slightly left at bulge. Easier
climbing to top.

7/11 Mourne Rambler
18m E1 (5b) Stelfox, Lawson, 1980
Start: 1m right of Sparrow. Climb the vertical crack, cross Hawk at
mid-height, and climb directly over the central bulge on good jugs.
Exit left below the top overhang.

Tormore Crag, right-hand wall. L = Landmark Boulder

7/12 Hawk

30m HVS (5a) Torrans, Sheridan, 1977
Start: This route takes the upper diagonal crack, starting opposite
Landmark Boulder. Climb bulge on flake jugs to ledge at foot of
corner. Traverse left along sloping ledge to reach start of diagonal
crack. Climb crack on good jugs and good protection to the bulge
above the yellow stain on Sparrow. Up and left to finish.

7/13 Maeve

18m VS (4b) Sheridan, Torrans, 1977
Route takes the obvious left-facing corner opposite Landmark
Boulder.
Start: As for Hawk. Climb bulge on flake jugs to small ledge at foot
of corner. Continue up corner on good holds to gain steep part of
corner above. Climb this by thin bridging moves (crux) to overlap.
Move left over overlap, easier climbing to top.

   About 7m right of Landmark Boulder there is a short corner at
the top of the crag, approached from the left by a short ramp. This is
Teach an Asail, VS (4b).

7/14 Deoch an Uasail

18m VS (4c) Somers, Goulding, 1975
Start: Immediately to the right of Teach an Asail. Climb easy
obvious crack, moving slightly right to reach crack at the side of
large left pointed block at about 7m. Move left until directly below a
short corner near the top of the crag which contains a small blunt
overhang. This corner is about 5m to the right of the top of Teach
an Asail. Climb straight up corner and exit.

   To the right of Deoch an Uasail there is an area of poor gullied
rock, followed by a steep section with its bulging headwall
underlined by a prominent horizontal crack. The next route starts
below the left-hand side of the horizontal crack.

Warthog, Tom Hand on the strenuous crux moves

7/15 Bedroom Boredom
24m HVS (5a) Somers, Goulding, Colton, 1975
Start: At base of thin twin vertical cracks. Climb parallel cracks to ledge and possible belay at 9m. Thinly traverse right, using horizontal crack for hands. Finish up a steep blocky groove.

Hawk. The Climber is Tom Ryan

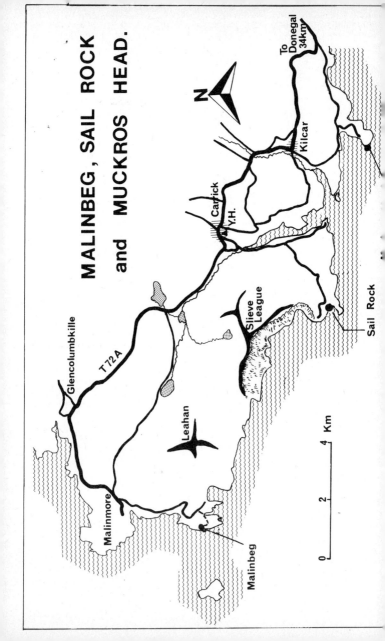

MALINBEG, SAIL ROCK and MUCKROS HEAD.

N

To Donegal 34Km
Kilcar
Carrick
Y.H.
Glencolumbkille
T72A
Malinmore
Malinbeg
Leahan
Slieve League
Sail Rock

0   2   4 Km

8 Muckros Head, Donegal
GR 162373 Sheet 3, ½″ Series

Introduction The cliff is composed of horizontally bedded sandstone. In between the layers of sandstone there are thin bands of mudstone which have eroded back more quickly, undercutting the sandstone layers. Consequently the more resistant sandstones have produced the numerous characteristic overhangs on the cliff. This crag is usually visited on day trips when the main mountain crags of Donegal are water-logged. The climbing is steep and strenuous, but the holds are usually large. The rock is sound, although the last metre or so can be a bit loose.

Access The crag is approached from Killybegs along the T72. After 7 km, fork left along the coast road (via Shalwy). Continue along this road for about 3 km, then take a small road on the left leading down to the low-lying Muckros headland. The road eventually degenerates into an untarred track, which you follow to a small car-park. From here a path leads down to a wave-cut platform and the left-hand end of the cliff. This platform is partially tidal.

Accommodation The area is remote, and camping is possible anywhere on the clifftop. Hotel/guest house accommodation is available in Killybegs.

8/1 Scut
11m E2 (5c) Somers, Torrans, 1978
Start: 3m right of the first corner on the crag below a short roof with crack in it. Move up and climb the roof. Gain the crack above with difficulty.

8/2 An Raibh Tu ar an gCarraig
15m HS (4b) Somers, 1977
Start: Route takes the obvious corner line right of Scut. Climb the corner.

Muckros Head, looking back along the tidal platform (p. 125)

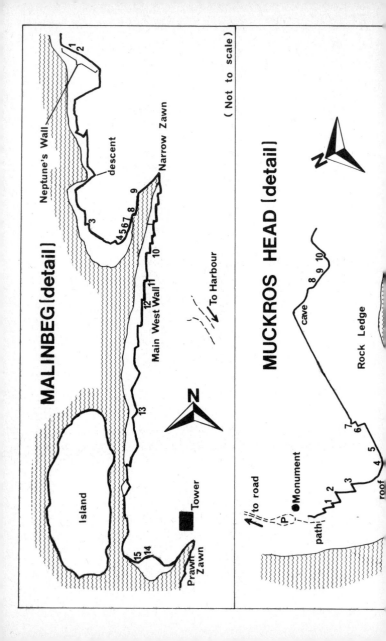

MALINBEG (detail)

Neptune's Wall

descent

Narrow Zawn

Main West Wall

To Harbour

Island

Tower

Prawn Zawn

(Not to scale)

MUCKROS HEAD (detail)

cave

Rock Ledge

roof

Monument

to road

path

P

8/3 Bombay Duck

15m S (4a) Higgs, Torrans, 1977
Start: At base of first corner left of the big roof. Climb small
overhang by wide bridging and good jams, and move up into corner.
Step across left to gain good ledge. Move up and climb wide crack to
top. Nut belay.

8/4 Tricky Dicky

17m VS (4c) Torrans, Higgs, 1977
Start: Below and to the right of the big roof— at the foot of arête.
Climb just left of bulging arête (awkward) to right end of roof.
Move right and climb edge of wall end of roof. Move right and climb
edge of wall above. Exit left and belay in back of recess.

8/5 Cois Farraige

18m VS (4c) Somers, Colton, 1977
Start: 3m right of Tricky Dicky there is a steep undercut wall with a
stepped crack up the centre. Starting holds are hard to reach.

8/6 Morning Glory

17m HS (4b) Colton, Somers, 1977
Start: Directly beneath overhanging corner 6m right of Cois
Farraige. Climb overhanging wall on large holds to a ledge on left
beneath the corner. Climb this and exit up left.

8/7 The Barb

18m E1/2 (5b) Windrim, Higgs, 1978
Start: Below corner just right of Morning Glory. Climb the slightly
overhanging corner for 10m. Traverse the steep left wall to small
stance on arête. Move up and climb the overhang on the right
(crux), finishing steeply.

   To the right of The Barb there is a 50m-long wall capped by
overhangs, and to the right of this wall is a large wide cave with big
blocks scattered outside. The next route takes obvious ledges and
the wide crack at the right side of the cave.

Primula, Calvin Torrans on the crux moves above the small stance

8/8 Boho Dance

20m S (4a) Higgs, Matheson, 1977
Start: Just to the right of the first large cave at base of short groove.
Climb groove to ledge, make awkward mantelshelf moves to gain
long platform at 8m. Move to left end of platform and climb wide
crack to small ledge. Step right and finish up steep wall. Nut belay in
alcove just below top.

8/9 Froth

18m HS (4b) Torrans, Sheridan, 1978
Start: Just to the right of Boho Dance. Climb the short wall to deep
horizontal crack and up to small ledge. Move left and climb wall on
horizontal ribs. Finish up short corner.

8/10 Primula

18m VS (4c) Torrans, Sheridan, 1977
Start: To the right of Froth, 1m around the next corner; route takes
the obvious weakness through the overhangs. Climb overhangs to
stance at 7m. Move up the wall moving right then back left and up
to top.

9 Sail Rock, Donegal
GR 559750 Sheet 3, $\frac{1}{2}''$ Series

Introduction Sail Rock is a huge quartzite slab set amongst poor broken shales and basalt, containing one excellent route.

Access The 'sail' is 6 km south-west of Carrick and 4 km south-east of Slieve League. Take the new road up Slieve League, leaving it approximately 1 km below the car-park. Walk south towards the sea, following a vague track to a Martello tower. Before reaching the tower, scramble down left to a loose spur which is followed to a point 20m above the sea. Traverse into the rock basin below the 'sail'.

Accommodation As for Malinbeg.

9/1 Main Mast
69m E2 (5b/c) Scott, Shaw, Nichol (one point of aid on Pitch 2 and nine on Pitch 3), 1967; Cowan (two points of aid); Ryan, Manson, Prendergast (first free ascent); 1981
Start: This superb route takes the obvious diagonal crack up the centre of the wall from right to left.
1   **15m** From the shallow scoop ascend broken cracks and slabs to the basalt dyke.
2   **18m** From the dyke follow the crack up steeply and diagonally left. The crack is followed directly. An aid point originally used here to regain the crack after moving left on flakes. Bridge up between flakes to a small stance.
3   **36m** The crack gradually becomes too narrow for jamming and the angle becomes vertical.

10 Malinbeg, Donegal

GR 148379 Sheet 3, " Series (for maps, see pages 122 and 124)

Introduction Malinbeg is a quartzite cliff, ranging from 10m to 30m in height, around the headland beyond Malinbeg harbour. It provides a mix of steep walls and slabs with routes mainly in the lower grades. Some climbs are serious because of lack of protection, and while most are not affected by the tide, a rough sea can hinder climbing in some areas. However, the place is generally pervaded by a holiday atmosphere.

Access From Killybegs take the T72A to Carrick and continue to the junction about 5 km to the west. Take the road to Malinmore or follow the T72A on to Glencolumbcille and then to Malinmore. From here follow the coast road to the harbour. From the harbour follow the path over the headland to the tower. The various parts of the cliff are easily located from here. The crag can be roughly divided into four areas: the North End, Narrow Zawn Area, Main West Wall and Prawn Zawn.

Accommodation Climbers usually camp on the headland just beyond the harbour. Cottages may be rented in Malinbeg and in Glencolumbcille. The nearest youth hostel is in Carrick.

The most northerly section of the crag is formed by the steep, pock-marked Neptune's Wall, giving a number of good routes in the S–VS range. Approach is at low tide by the ledge below the wall. The two best routes are:

10/1 The Bosun's Ladder

15m S (4a) Sloane, O'Connor, Leonard, 1977
Start: Second crack from left-hand end of wall. Follow an obvious deep vertical crack and groove system with good holds. Crux at about 10m.

Sail Rock. Main Mast climbs, out of sight, to a belay (b) on the black band, then follows the obvious diagonal crack left to the top. The arête on the left is Roaring Forties, VS (4c)

10/2 Hydrophobia

15m VS (4b) Keena, Long, 1978
Start: 2m right of The Bosun's Ladder. Follow a direct line vertically up the centre of the wall on good holds. Mild in the grade.

The next series of routes are all reached from a flat terrace to the north and west of Narrow Zawn. Descent can be made down easy slabs at the southern end of the area to a flat terrace above high-water mark.

10/3 Calvin's Corner

8m VS (4b) Torrans, Billane, 1975
Start: At the right-hand end of the terrace is an obvious dark corner. The crack in the back of this is followed to the top. Mild in the grade. Difficulties are short.

Narrow Zawn Area

10/4 Shiver me Timbers

20m S (4a) Kinsella, Leonard, 1974
Start: From the large terrace the route takes the obvious chimney to steeper rock overlooking the Zawn. Climb the chimney and then gain some easier rock. Continue up to some cracks on the left, runner. Climb the bulging section using the cracks and some small holds (crux). Continue up easier rock to top.

10/5 Moby Dick

20m S (3c) Leonard, Kinsella, 1974
Start: A few metres to the right of Shiver me Timbers. Climb the groove on good footholds for about 5m. Step right on to an obvious small ledge and move on to steeper section over Zawn. Continue up on small good holds and crack on the left to easier rock on the top. Exposed.

Paula Turley climbing Moby Dick. The climber in the top left-hand corner is on the start of Lord of the Flies

10/6 The Bold Princess Royal
30m HVS (5a) McKenzie, Ryan, 1975
This is the steep ramp and corner halfway along the north side of
Narrow Zawn.
Start: On the wall below line of ramp. At 5m gain ramp proper
(delicate). Continue up to ledge at mid-way and good nut runner.
Climb from here on small bridging holds (protection hard to find
but some small nuts useful) until a strenuous pull up brings better
things and finish. Peg or nut belay.

10/7 Zimmerman Blues
30m VS (4c) Billane, Torrans, 1975
Start: The route takes a ramp from the water level which leads to a
deep obvious crack at mid-height a few metres to the right of The
Bold Princess Royal. Gain the ramp and move up to small
overhang. Move over this and climb the crack to the top.

At low tide it is possible to cross Narrow Zawn to reach:

10/8 Lord of the Flies
25m HS (4b) Walsh, Gargan (alternate leads), 1975
Start: A few metres left of Flying Enterprise. Climb an obvious
weakness in the wall to gain a ramp. Gain the upper ramp at top by
stretchy mantelshelf. Possible belay at top of obvious black
chimney. Just right of this climb the obvious layback crack which is
a feature of the cliff (crux) and up steep ground to finish.

From Lord of the Flies traverse along the base of the cliff to reach
the **Main West Wall**.

The Bold Princess Royal. The climber is Ken Higgs

10/9   10/10

10/9 Flying Enterprise
27m VS (4c) Ryan, McKenzie, 1975
This excellent route takes a line up to the two right-trending ramps on the smooth wall. The route first gains the lower ramp and then the upper one by a short wall.
Start: At a groove which leads to the base of the lower ramp. Climb the groove on to a ledge at 5m. From its left end climb a short wall (crux) to a ledge and then diagonally right up the ramp to the top. Mild in grade.

10/10 Fiddler's Green
27m HVS (5a) Walsh, Webster, 1978
Start: The route takes the wide ramp about 3m right of Flying Enterprise. Gain the ramp at 7m by some strenuous moves and follow ramp right to foot of vertical corner (belay taken on first ascent). Ascend the corner above until it is possible to gain the sloping ledge on the right (crux). Good nut runners.

10/11 The Wreck of the Mary Deare
27m VS (4c) Ryan, McKenzie, 1975
Start: The route takes an obvious corner which overhangs nearly directly opposite the northern end of the island. Climb the corner and traverse left under first overhang. Continue up the corner to finish — hard. A superb climb.

Prawn Zawn
Descent is by abseil down the obvious centre section on to a large ledge below the promontory which runs between the Zawn and the island channel. Nut anchors are difficult to establish and pegs may be found useful.

Flying Enterprise and Fiddler's Green

10/12 Pieces of Eight
20m E1 (5b) McKenzie, Kerr (one aid point), 1976; Torrans (first free ascent), 1978
This climb takes the thin crack which splits the smooth wall about 5m left of usual descent.

10/13 John Dory
22m S (4a) Leonard, Walsh, 1975
Start: From the ledge below the abseil point, this is the obvious crack on the left-hand side of the central depression under a small overhang. Bridge out over the overhang and climb the vertical crack above on good holds until the angle relents, and continue to the top on small but adequate holds.

11 Lough Belshade, Donegal

GR 974899 Sheet 3, $\frac{1}{2}''$ Series

Introduction Lough Belshade is enclosed by a series of granite crags from 20m to 100m in height, all offering excellent climbing. The climbs described lie on the main crag (Belshade Buttress) but many good short routes can be found on the smaller outcrops to the right and below this buttress. Lough Belshade provides perfect granite giving scope for a wide variety of techniques from open-slab climbing to strenuous jamming cracks. Protection varies but is usually adequate, and the situations are always impressive. There is a feeling of isolation and remoteness, in very beautiful countryside.

Access From Donegal Town a well-signposted road leads to the top of Lough Eske. Alternatively, the same spot can be reached from Ballybofey/Donegal road (T18). Here a minor road branches off the Lough Eske loop, ending in a group of farm buildings. It is possible to leave cars here. A way-marked path leads past the Doonan Waterfall and continues up the river valley beyond. Follow the first major river entering from the left to reach the Lough, and then follow the shore to the obvious beach at the northern end. About $1\frac{1}{2}$ hours from the road in normal conditions, although after heavy rain the route becomes rather tediously wet.

Accommodation An excellent camp site is found on the lake shore just below the crag; and 40m from the shore is a superb gite, under the obvious large boulder, which can take up to four.

11/1 Byzantium

122m VS (4b,4a,4b,4a,4a) Winder, Hill, 1954
The lower section gives some very good climbing, but after Pitch 3 it tends to become rather rambling.
Start: This route takes a line up the buttress of rock bounding the left side of the main face. Below the buttress, almost at the lake, a 70m slab tongue leads to the foot of the crag. This may be climbed (VD), or avoided on the left to reach a good platform below a steep groove.

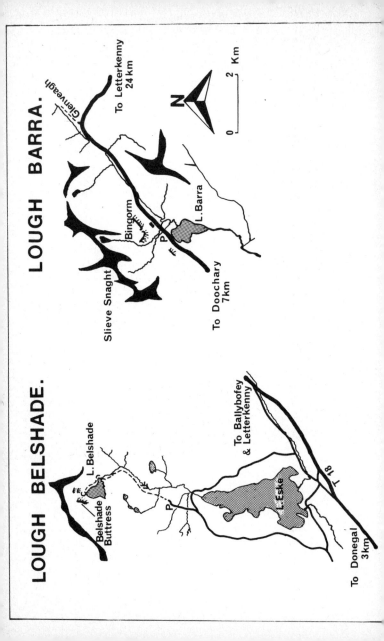

LOUGH BELSHADE.

L. Belshade

Belshade
Buttress

To Ballybofey
& Letterkenny

L. Eske

T 18

To Donegal
3 km

P

LOUGH BARRA.

Glenveagh

To Letterkenny
24 km

Slieve Snaght

Bingorm

P

L. Barra

To Doochary
7 km

N

0   2

Km

1   17m Climb the groove, moving left on to a vegetated ledge at 14m. Back right to belay.

2   27m Ascend the corner groove above, exiting left at the top. Move diagonally right and up past vegetation to large block on wall on the left.

3   20m Move left across the block and up the groove above (crux). Follow a good crack left at the top to ledge.

4   28m Climb groove above to the second of two ledges.

5   30m Move right across the slab above to a crack overhanging at the bottom. Climb this and the groove above. Follow a rib on the right to the top.

11/2 Classical Revival

82m E1 (4b,5b,5a) Stelfox, MacPherson, Rea, 1981

This route takes the obvious curving ramp leading up to a large overhang at the left-hand side of the face, providing two excellent pitches in a very impressive situation.

Start: As for Byzantium.

1   17m As for Byzantium.

2   38m From belay move up to the base of heather-filled corner on the right. Step right on to the arête and airily swing round on to the wall to gain a good crack. Follow this up to the corner from where diagonal cracks and a narrow ramp lead with increasing difficulty across the smooth open slab. About 3m below the large overhang, belay on a small ledge below a good crack.

3   28m Climb the crack, swinging past the overhang on excellent holds. Continue up the corner above. Finish by the arête on the left, or the awkward chimney above.

Lough Belshade, main face: a = approach route to route 11/3 and 11/4; d marks descent; and x is the position photographed in the following picture (p. 141)

Ian Rea on one of the smaller buttresses at Lough Belshade – marked x in the previous picture

11/3 Lest We Forget
75m HVS (4b,4c,5a) Stelfox, Rea, 1982
A very enjoyable route taking a more or less direct line up the
centre of the crag.
Start: As for Land of Heart's Desire.
1   39m Follow small ledges trending left to reach the ledge at the
foot of the obvious crack system, which leads to the top of the crag.
Gain crack and follow with increasing difficulty to gain grass ledge
and belay, below large flake.
2   18m Move up for 3m and step left on to slab. Follow the crack
to the small perched ledge in the niche under the roof.
3   18m Bridge around roof and gain twin cracks which split the
slab. Bridge up these with only one difficult move, to gain another
small niche. Friends essential for protection. Continue up the crack
to the top.

11/4 Land of Heart's Desire
83m HVS (5a,5a,5a,4c) Rea, Stelfox, 1981
Start: This route, giving sustained, good quality climbing, takes the
prominent corner system up the right side of the main face. Access
to the start is by the huge sloping heather ledge which is gained
immediately right of the slab tongue below Byzantium.
1   18m Climb short steep wall just right of a small, subsidiary
corner at the top end of the heather ledge. After 5m follow the
obvious traverse right, to gain the huge block at the base of the main
corner system.
2   35m Climb corner directly to reach a perfect belay ledge just
left of twin cracks in the next corner.
3   26m Make a few moves up a small corner, then swing right into
the twin cracks. Up these to base of final steep corner. Up this to
belay on large grassy ledge on the left.
4   4m Up the short layback above — then up grass and easy rock
to belay far back.

Lest We Forget, Ian Rea on the second pitch, first ascent

12 Lough Barra, Donegal
GR 9313 Sheets 1 + 3, ½" Series

Introduction The area generally referred to as Lough Barra is composed of five separate cliffs on the south flank of Slieve Snaght, above the lake that gives the crag its name. The best climbing is to be found on Bingorm West — the cleanest and most continuous area of rock directly above the only house on the north side of the road. The most characteristic feature is the huge, central square-cut gully. Lough Barra gives some of the best granite climbing in Ireland, mainly on steep short slabs and bulges with few cracks. Traditionally pegs have been used and many are still in place, but the normal selection of chocks should suffice.

Access From Letterkenny take the L74 west for 7 km to a road junction. Take the right-hand fork (L82) in the direction of Churchill and then a left turn a further 7 km on, signposted for Doocharry. After 15 km of mountainous terrain this road begins to drop into the Owenree river valley. About 8 km from Doocharry Lough Barra appears on the left and the crags on the right. Cars can be parked at the bridge just down the road from the farmhouse. From here a small track follows the stream to the left of the crag. Follow this to get above the valley bog, then trend rightwards up the hill to the base of the central gully. About 20 minutes from the road.

Accommodation Climbers usually camp at small roadside sites between Doocharry and Lough Barra — permission should be sought if close to a farm. Provisions are available in Doocharry.

Lough Barra – view from road above farmhouse. S marks Square-cut Gully; D = Delta Face; T = Thin Gully; d = descent routes

12/1 Diversion

133m S (4a) Kenny, Winder 1955

Start: About 40m left of the lowest section of rock to the left of Square-Cut Gully there is a rib that comes particularly low, with a large boulder below it. The climb starts up the rib but then breaks right to continue in a straight line to the top.

1   **30m** Climb the rib slanting left, then up vegetation to the base of the next rib.

2   **20m** Continue straight up. At 15m pull up into a mossy groove to the right of a recess with mossy walls. Climb left on to vegetation and ascend above the recess to flake belay.

3   **26m** Straight up, with one hard mantelshelf, to patch of vegetation on the left of a vertical strip of vegetation. Peg belay.

4   **27m** Cross strip of vegetation and ascend rib going slightly right to jammed blocks. Climb these to belay.

5   **24m** Mixed scrambling to belay below corner.

6   **6m** Climb corner to top.

12/2 Triversion

98m S (3c) Healy, Winder, 1956

Start: As for Diversion, but follow the rib to the left.

1   **40m** Follow the rib up and left to vegetation. Move up slabs, diagonally left to the base of the obvious pockled wall and corner.

2   **28m** Climb the pockled wall, moving out left at the top to reach a ledge at 16m. Continue up to belay on a large vegetated platform.

3   **22m** Descend 2m and move right to a quartzite horizontal fault. Traverse along this easily, though exposed, to a large overhang. Step down and around this to belay on a huge block.

4   **8m** Move right and up to heather and finish, or ascend the clean corner above (4a) stepping left near the top.

The next four routes lie on the Delta Face — a clean, inverted triangle of rock to the right of Square-Cut Gully.

Triversion, Robert Bankhead on the third pitch

12/3 Lazarus

60m VS (4c,4a) O'Halpin, Moloney (alternate leads), 1962
Start: 9m up subsidary gully to right of Square-Cut Gully. Route
starts up the ramp which runs from right of gully, just below and left
of a black streaked wall.

1   30m Climb initial bulge using crack on right and continue up
wall of ramp to heather ledge. Climb wall behind ledge for 2m and
move delicately left to edge. Climb arête to heather ledge and belay.
2   30m Move up edge of rib and step right into chimney.
Continue up and out right over white slab to heather ramp, moving
diagonally left to belay.

12/4 Gethsemane

84m E1 (5a,4c,4c,4c) Griffin, Curran (one aid point), 1973
This climb takes a direct line up the centre of the Delta Face.
Start: At an obvious white recess below the apex of the Delta Face.

1   33m Climb the slanting groove in the recess from right to left
until stopped by overhangs. Make a difficult pull out left over the
overhangs to a resting place below a very steep wall. Climb the
crack in the wall, using a sling to exit on to the Delta Face. Climb up
easily for 5m to belay on Larceny, Pitch 2.
2   24m Straight up short layback pitch as for Larceny, but instead
of traversing left go straight up to the smooth walls and climb
delicately right into a scoop with small spike runner. Move up to
reach heather and easy rock which is followed to block belay to top
of Pitch 3 of Larceny.
3   21m Step right and climb easily to the foot of an obvious
corner. Bridge over the first bulge and continue to the second where
a move right is made on to the arête in a fine position. Make a
difficult move up into a scoop and delicately back left to continue
more easily up the arête to a good ledge and belay below the final
short corner.
4   6m Climb this deceptive corner to the top.

Delta Face of Lough Barra: S marks Square-cut Gully

12/5 Aiseiri

109m VS (4c,4a,4b,4a) Goulding, O'Leary (alternate leads), 1960
The main feature of the Delta Face is an overhang running
diagonally right from its V-shaped lowest point.
Start: 9m to right of this, about 4m below and to right of vegetated
niche.

1   30m Climb 3m straight up to sloping ledge. Follow this as it
rises steeply to left, then make a tricky move into vegetated niche.
Continue up left and after 3m move out right across vegetated rake
to rib leading diagonally left. Follow this to below overhang. Make
two awkward moves across the right-hand wall to vegetation. Move
back left on to the Delta Face to a stance above the overhang.

2   18m Layback up groove and follow obvious line of weakness
around corner on left and continue up with steep wall on right to
belay.

3   24m Follow groove for 4m to good flake runner. Step up on to
slab and traverse left to edge. Pull around corner and continue up to
triangular overhang on right where it is possible to regain the
groove. Belay.

4   37m Pull out right and across vegetated rake, then up obvious
groove to belay.

12/6 Larceny

128m VS (4b,4a,4b,4b,4a) Kenny, Laracy, 1955
Start: From the lowest point of the cliff to the right of Square-Cut
Gully an obvious ramp is followed which leads diagonally left, up
vegetation and rock, to the bottom apex of Delta Face.

1   60m There is a tricky corner about halfway up the pitch, and
about 6m above this there is a short steep wall to be surmounted.

2   9m From top of ramp move round left on to a ledge at bottom
of Delta Face. Follow ledge for about 6m and belay at bottom of
groove.

3   24m As for Pitch 3 of Aiseiri.

4   8m Retrace steps about 3m to point where it is possible to
climb a straight overhanging wall on right using crack. Climb wall
and step on to open slabs of Delta Face proper. Ascend diagonally
right to obvious triangle block lying at foot of steep corner.

5   **27m** Descend about 3m and climb out right. Climb up for about 6m and then traverse diagonally left above belay. Cross a slab towards left edge of Delta Face — some delicate and exposed moves — and finish up groove.

12/7 Tarquin's Groove
108m HS (4b,4a,4a,4a,4a) Winder, Drasdo (alternate leads), 1955
Consistently good climbing with varied situations. The route takes the obvious steep groove to the left of Thin Gully — Risorgiomento, VS. The line of the groove can be followed down by eye, vertically at first and then diagonally across the vegetation and rock rib.
Start: Where the line of the groove meets the sharply sloping foot of the cliff about 6m to the right of the start of Aiseiri. Alternatively, and possibly more satisfactorily, the normal start for Larceny may be followed to just above the awkward corner halfway up.
1   **27m** Climb to base of groove as for Larceny. Belay at rowan tree.
2   **24m** Climb the groove by handholds on the left wall. Climb the black wall and exit left to holly tree belay.
3   **16m** Ascend the steep wall on the right and move left to base of long crack.
4   **19m** Climb crack to belay on large ledge beneath overhangs on right.
5   **22m** Traverse left at overhang and ascend bulge. Cross on to slab above on the right of the corner and finish up easier rock.

12/8 Surplomb Grise
136m VS (-,4c,4a,-,4b) Winder, Bell, 1955
Start: About 30m to the right of Thin Gully (and about halfway between it and the obvious prominent corner of Rule Britannia) is a long straight steep groove. Directly beneath this, the lines of vegetation reach the highest point at a large overhanging cap of heather. The crux lies about 9m above, and slightly to the left of, this heather.
1   **75m** Climb the mixed rock and vegetation in the lower half of Thin Gully and then traverse right to ledge at top of heather cap.
2   **22m** The crux: climb two short slabs above, trending left, then move left and climb a steep crack leading on to a small pulpit. Avoid

bulge above by moving out right — delicate — and up to ledge.
Continue up to corner on right. Good thread belay.

3   **18m** Move left across groove and climb steep crack to trees.

4   **9m** Climb generally left until the top of an enormous block
projecting over the gully is reached.

5   **12m** Climb a short wall to the base of a vertical groove above
and slightly right. Substantial holds in the groove lead to easier rock
and the top.

12/9 Rule Britannia/Erin go Bragh

*79m HVS (5a,3c,5a,5a) Banner, O'Neill (Pitches 1 and 2), 1961;
Ingram, Goulding (Pitches 3 and 4), 1962*
Rule Britannia was given a more direct finish after Pitch 2 — Erin
go Bragh.
Start: About halfway between Thin Gully and Fomorian there is a
prominent corner which is about as far to the right of Surplomb
Grise as the latter route is right of Thin Gully. The length of the
climb does not include initial scrambling.

1   **21m** Start from a large grassy area below the corner. Climb up
zigzag gangways, moving to the left at first, then right, then left
again until the rock becomes steeper. Climb the next 3m with
difficulty to a sloping ledge. Traverse left across wet streaks — thin
— to reach the bottom of the grass, up right to belay.

2   **13m** Up the slab on the left to another grassy ledge and along
this for about 7m to a small spike belay.

3   **27m** From the holly tree move left 3m. Climb to a corner and
up it to an overhang. Move right and up to flake. Step left to a nose
and continue up to overhanging corner.

4   **18m** Turn overhang by climbing up right-hand wall. Easy
climbing to belay.

12/10 Calvary Crossings

84m VS (4c,4c,4c) Griffin, Curran, 1973
Start: This climb takes the area of rock left of the first belay on
Ploughshare to finish above the large prominent corner, which in
turn lies directly above the first pitch of Rule Britannia.

1   **36m** Climb the first pitch of Ploughshare, taking the lower of
the two starts.

Tarquin's Groove, Sheila Willis on the black wall of Pitch 2.

2   39m Climb diagonally left across the slab, passing a good flake runner until a few delicate moves lead to the crack line emerging from the large corner mentioned above. Move up to a small heather ledge and bridge the corner above to the top, leaving it to the right by memorable moves. Up more easily to a small grotto and thread belays.

3   9m Up the crack above the cave and over a small overhang (wet) to the top; belay well back.

12/11 Ploughshare
62m VS (4c,4a,4a) Healy, O'Halpin (alternate leads), 1961
Start: Situated in the centre of the main face.

1   22m From the highest (left hand) end of the strip of vegetation, climb diagonally upwards using thin flakes and friction. A short steep wall is followed by a delicate traverse on a horizontal ledge. Up to vegetation and belay.

2   18m Traverse right for 10m on broken rock to a pocked slab on the left.

3   22m Continue upwards, using a series of platforms moving right, then left, to avoid a small overhang. Continue up on vegetated platforms, moving left where the walls fall away to a slab. Climb the corner of the slab and finish up a short wall.

12/12 Fomorian
65m HS (4b,4a,3b) Healy, Winder, 1960
Start: Halfway between Surplomb Grise and the end of the cliff, left of a prominent overhanging slab low down, directly beneath an obvious fault slanting left.

1   23m Climb curving corner for about 12m. Step right easily before vegetation. Climb steep slab to gain vegetated terrace.

2   21m Traverse right along ledge for 4m and then climb diagonally left to weakness in overhang. Continue up to grassy ledge.

3   21m Easy climbing leads to the top.

13 Fair Head, Antrim
GR 1743 Sheet 5: 1:50,000

Introduction The cliffs at Fair Head are formed from a sill of dolerite some 70m thick intruded into carboniferous sediments. The cooling of the dolerite in columnar form has produced the characteristic vertical crack and chimney structure. The cliffs are two miles long, mainly vertical, and from 30m to 90m high. The routes invariably follow crack lines, giving excellent sustained jamming and bridging with ever-available protection.

There are well over one hundred routes on the crag, and all but a handful are of exceptional quality. The majority included here tend to cluster around the two descent gullies, although the few longer routes in the centre of the crag demand attention.

Access Take the A2 out of Ballycastle towards Cushendun and Cushendall. At Ballyvoy follow the signpost left to Fair Head, eventually arriving at the National Trust car-park at Coolanlough. For the Grey Man's Path descent, follow the way-marked path from here to where it veers parallel to the crag. Gain the cliff edge at the obvious gap bridged by a unique fallen column.

For the Ballycastle descent gully, turn left along a small road before reaching Coolanlough and park at the cattle grid at the farm entrance. Follow the low wall leading seaward to a small stile. Cross this and walk uphill until Lough Doo comes into sight. Contour around the lake to its northern end, from where a small stream flows down the Ballycastle descent gully.

Accommodation The area between Murlough Bay and the Grey Man's Path is National Trust property and camping is not permitted. North of this, the local farmers should be asked. Nearest official camp sites, youth hostel and hotels are in Ballycastle. The Dalriada CC usually has use of a hut in the vicinity, but prior contact with the club secretary is necessary (see p. 19).

Grey Man's Path area
The routes are described looking from left to right below the crag.

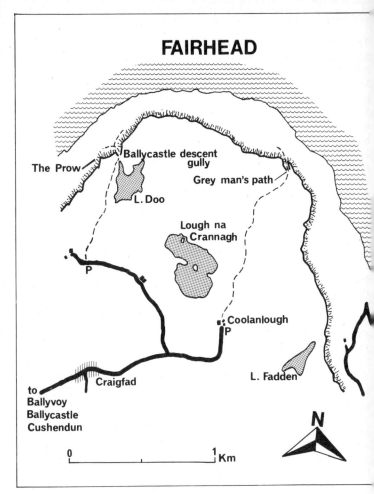

FAIRHEAD

The Prow

Ballycastle descent gully

Grey man's path

L. Doo

Lough na Crannagh

P

Coolanlough
P

Craigfad

L. Fadden

to
Ballyvoy
Ballycastle
Cushendun

0   1 Km

N

Descend the Grey Man's Path and follow a small path around the bottom of the cliff to the right. At the left end of the cliff, where the good rock deteriorates into steep vegetated shale, there has been a rock fall. The first route takes the corner to the right of this.

13/1 December
55m VS (4c,4c) McHugh, McKenzie, 1968
An interesting and well-protected route.
Start: By scrambling into the cavern at the base of the corner groove.
1   **25m** From the base of the corner climb the crack (difficulty at 6m) and emerge into daylight. Continue pleasantly up the corner to a belay niche.
2   **30m** Continue up to a ledge, followed by a chimney. Advance to a sizeable overhang which is surmounted using good holds. Easier rock leads to the top.

13/2 Duais
42m E1 (5b) McDermott, Rodgers, 1969
A strenuous but well-protected route.
Start: The next obvious corner right of December. Ascend the corner crack to a sloping platform at 12m. It is possible to belay here. Continue up the corner past three overhangs, the last being the hardest.

13/3 Poor Relation
45m E1 (4a,5b) Rotherham, Rowe (one aid point), 1976; Torrans, Sheridan (first free ascent), 1979
Start: As for Duais.
1   **12m** Ascend the corner to the sloping ledge as for Duais.
2   **33m** Move up to overhang. Traverse right for 3m to a shallow groove and crack. Layaway up crack to reach poor jams (crux). Pull up on to slab and traverse left to corner crack, which is difficult to start.

3/4 Doldrum

2m E1 (4c,5b,4c) McHugh, Heffernan, 1968

About 100m right of the previous routes, the leftward-slanting overhanging crack of Curser, HVS, marks the start of Rathlin Wall. The deep gash running up the centre of this wall is Clarion, VS. Doldrum takes the crackline between these two routes. Attractive in its directness and increasing exposure, this route provides a sustained level of interest.

Start: Immediately left of the huge boulder which lies against the crag.

1   22m Ascend the cracks diagonally left to a secure perch below the band of overhangs.

2   45m Move up the obvious chimney until it is possible to pull out left and gain the top of a large flake. Step right to off-width crack. Proceed with difficulty until at 6m the chimney relents a little, and continue up twin cracks to a minute stance. From here step right and layback for 6m to stance.

3   5m Move left to spillikin. Climb the obvious crack behind the spillikin to the top. Or climb deep cracks directly behind the belay.

3/5 Hurricane

63m E2 (5b,5b) McHugh, O'Brien (two aid points), 1969; Torrans first free ascent), 1974

Start: A difficult and serious climb with plenty of exposure, this route takes the next obvious line right of Clarion.

1   45m Climb the groove until at 12m a niche is reached. Exit from the niche and continue up the crack to an overhang (crux). Climb overhang on hand jams. With little less difficulty, proceed up the vertical jam crack for 7m until it eases. Take an airy belay at the top of the shattered pillar. If not leading through, the second should belay at the base of the pillar.

2   18m From the top of the pillar, traverse left and continue up the vertical crack above to the top.

Left wall of Grey Man's Path from Toby Jug to Sreang Scuab

13/6 Toby Jug

55m E1 (5a,5b) Torrans, Cowan (four aid points), 1970; Torrans, Sheridan (first free ascent), 1976

Start: The right-hand boundary of Rathlin Wall is the large corner gully of Greencorner, HS. The large corner to the right of this is Darth Vadar Lives, HVS. To the right again is Serem, HVS, a loose prominent groove. There is a huge corner to the right of Serem. Toby Jug takes the crack a few metres to the left of this.

1   **33m** Climb the crack weaving left then right to join the main crack. Proceed with difficulty to belay on ledge.

2   **22m** Climb crack to small overhang. Move left to foot of leaning corner. Up corner on excellent jams.

The next two routes share the same start at the foot of the huge corner to the right of Toby Jug.

13/7 The Brasser

46m E2 (5c,5b) Torrans, Sheridan (one aid point), 1978; Murphy (first free ascent), 1983

1   **36m** Climb corner by bridging and jamming, passing good spike runner on the left. Continue up corner with increasing difficulty to reach foot of groove. Layback crack and pull into groove on poor jams (crux). Continue up crack on poor jams to reach good jams and up to belay ledge.

2   **10m** Layback up corner to reach ledge on left. Awkward to top.

13/8 Sandpiper

42m E2 (5c,5a) Torrans, Sheridan (one aid point), 1976; Lawson (first free ascent), 1980

Start: As for The Brasser at the foot of the corner.

1   **36m** Climb the corner to the bottom of the difficult groove of The Brasser and make a difficult step right to finger cracks on the right wall. Up cracks, which get wider, to belay on ledge above the narrow chimney of Striapach.

2   **6m** Climb the difficult crack above.

Grey Man's Path area: G indicates the path

13/9 Striapach
56m HVS (4c,5a,5a) Goulding, Ingram, 1968
This is the obvious chimney about 75m right of Greencorner
formed by a large flake. It gives a superb, though poorly protected,
36m pitch of chimneying.
Start: Up the twin cracks.
1   14m At the top of the cracks step left around the corner and
negotiate the steep step. Enter the chimney and belay.
2   36m Ascend the chimney (very strenuous). A resting place is
available on the left arête shortly before the most difficult section.
Exit left from the chimney and belay on the chockstone.
3   6m Climb the difficult crack above.

13/10 Jolly Rodger
*68m E3 (6a,5c), Manson, Codling (one aid point), 1981; Codling
(first free ascent), 1982*
Start: The next large corner right of Striapach contains Orange
Blossom Special, E1 (5b). To the left of this is a steep smooth wall,
split by two cracks, the right-hand one of which is characterised by a
jammed block at its top. Jolly Rodger takes the left-hand crack.
1   23m Climb up to a small black overhang below crack, pass
overhang on the right, using good holds, and step back left to *in-situ*
peg. Step up to gain thin crack which is climbed with increasing
difficulty to good jug. Up easier ground to belay on small ledge.
2   45m Continue up the crack, passing a few bulges on the way, in
a fine situation.

13/11 Sreang Scuab
45m E2 (4b,5b) Lawson, Derbyshire, 1980
This route takes the obvious steep groove with three small
overhangs to the right of Orange Blossom Special.
Start: At jammed blocks below groove.
1   9m Climb to right-hand side of blocks. One awkward move
leads to ledge below groove.

Hurricane, Tommy Maguire on the crux moves in the niche of Pitch 1

2   36m Climb up easily to first overhang and surmount this on excellent jams (crux). Continue up until it is possible to bridge on to cracked left wall. Move up by bridging and jamming to shallow chimney, passing a sound hollow flake. Exit from chimney into off-width. One hard move to reach good spike. Continue up blocks to top.

13/12 Burn Up
75m HVS (5a,5a,5a) McHugh, Billane, 1970
A superb route offering good situations and an airy aspect.
Start: This route follows the first obvious groove right of the Grey Man's Path.
1   39m Enter the groove and ascend to the overhang which is taken direct (awkward). Climb on up to a throne belay on the left.
2   31m Proceed with increasing difficulty until a commodious ledge is reached on the right.
3   5m Step back left into the crack and layback hurriedly to the top.

13/13 Born to Run
75m E4 (6a,5c,5c) Cooper, Manson (one aid point), 1982; Murphy, Ryan (first free ascent), 1983
Continuing round the crag from Burn Up, pass two narrow cracked walls, and a grassier section, to reach a steep wall containing an obvious chimney with a huge overhang at ¾-height: 7m right of this is a thin crack rising from an overhang.
Start: At the foot of the wall below this.
1   30m Climb cracked wall and corner until possible to move right to a flake. Using this climb to below the roof. Climb the roof and the crack above to a ledge, then continue up the crack to a flake and belay on a good small ledge above.
2   18m Continue up to a large flake-formed crack. Up this until possible to move left up to a ledge. Climb a series of small ledges to a semi-hanging belay below an obvious finger crack.
3   27m Up the finger crack until possible to follow a diagonal fault right to a groove. Climb this with difficulty until possible to move right to a ledge. Gain a higher ledge and continue on good jams and layback holds to a ledge just below the top. Continue easily to top.

Toby Jug, Ken Higgs on the final crack of the second pitch

13/14 New City Allstars
66m E1 (5b,5b,5a) Smith, Cole (one rest point), 1980; Torrans, Stelfox, Sheridan (first free ascent), 1980
Start: At a steep crack on the right side of the deep incut bay about 300m from the Grey Man's Path.
1   24m Climb the crack and chimney to the first overhang. Surmount this and continue up to the ledge using a few holds on the right.
2   27m Climb the awkward jamming groove/chimney (crux) to the second overhang. Traverse left and continue up the exposed wall on small holds — becoming easier — to a ledge.
3   15m Climb the delightful jamming crack above, which widens into a chimney.

13/15 Scarecrow
100m HVS (5a,4c,5a) McKenzie, McGrath, 1981
Start: At the foot of the second crack system on the seaward face right of New City Allstars.
1   35m Ascend wide corner on good jams and bridging. Belay on large ledge on left.
2   35m Continue up the cracks above until an exit right can be made on to an exposed small belay.
3   30m Climb the airy off-width above by many and various tactics (crux). Continue up the easy chimney above to the top.

Ballycastle descent gully area
Routes are described from left to right, looking at the crag after descent. After ten minutes' walk from the gully, moving left, you pass a huge leaning boulder. Just beyond this boulder the path rises to a small col between another large boulder and the crag. The deep groove which starts on the col is Cuchulainn. The corner on the right with the boulder-choked chimney is Viking, VS (rather loose), and the rightward-slanting crack 3m to the left is Roaring Meg. A further five minutes' walk leads to a 12m-high detached column shaped like a sabre-tooth. 150m left of this is a group of columns,

Born to Run, Martin Manson on the first ascent

b

b

b

b

b

13/17

13/16

40m high, leaning against the cliff. The largest of these, with a bridging flake on top, is taken by An Bealach Rhunda. Just left of this, the upper half of the crag is characterised by a big open corner facing right. This ends mid-way in a grassy terrace, the right-hand end of which is reached by a crack/groove system, forming the line of:

13/16 An Gobán Saor
90m E1 (5a,4c,5b) Somers, Hand, 1979
1   **30m** Climb the crack with continuous bridging on the right. Belay on a good ledge above the crack.
2   **21m** Continue up the groove to an entertaining chockstone and move out left. Reach the terrace and cross it to a belay at the foot of the corner.
3   **39m** Climb the corner to reach an inhospitable little niche 5m below the top. Move out right (crux) to a flat ledge, allowing a higher ledge to be reached. Continue easily to top.

13/17 An Bealach Rhunda
112m E1 (4c,5b,4a,4c) Torrans, Sheridan, 1976
Start: At the foot of the crack to the right of a small detached column.
1   **52m** Climb the crack and chimney to a ledge at 12m. Move left to climb the crack between the main column and the wall. Chimney up this, passing a ledge on the right at 36m. Continue up with a slight increase in difficulty to a good ledge on the right.
2   **30m** Move back into the chimney and airily gain the top of the column and flake. Go across the flake on to the wall, which is climbed with one awkward move to reach a small ledge on the right. Ignoring the corner to the right, climb the short wall on the left above, moving in from the right (crux). Continue up the thin crack to a wide ramp and a ledge. Climb a short awkward groove on the right to reach a large ramp running up left to good ledge.

The lines of An Gobán Saor and An Bealach Rhunda in the middle of the main crag: b = belay points

3   24m Climb ramp and make an awkward move left to small ledges. Up right to corner crack, which is followed to belay on ledge.
4   6m Climb steep crack up the final wall, hard to start.

The next routes lie immediately to the east of Roaring Meg and are reached by scrambling up the grassy terraces sloping up from left to the large block. 70m left of the block is the deep chimney of Herbivore, HVS, starting at half-height. The obvious pod-shaped groove right of this is:

13/18 The Vandals
57m E1 (5c,5b) Buckley, Barrett, 1979
Start: Scramble up the rock and heather and belay on the right just below the pod.
1   21m Move into the pod and climbing with increasing difficulty up the crack, reach holds on the left wall (crux) enabling one to continue up and leftwards to small ledge.
2   36m The groove above is followed to the top of the cliff.

13/19 Easy Rider/Aifric
80m E2 (4c,5c,5c) Cooper, Manson (Pitch 1), Sheridan, Torrans (Pitches 2, 3), 1980
Start: 5m to the right of the left end of the huge overhang splitting the crag right of The Vandals. The climb takes a traverse line from right to left under the overhang, finishing up a short crack.
1   30m Climb corner to a ledge below the overhang. Climb this and step right to a finger crack which is followed to large crack and grassy ledge. Step right to a thin crack and continue to belay at foot of corner below overhang.
2   35m Up corner crack to overhang and traverse left. After 1m step down on to a narrow ledge which peters out. A very delicate step past bulge (crux) to foothold out on left which eventually leads to better holds. Across and down slightly to ledges and up to belay.
3   15m Climb the crack in right wall.

The main wall of Fair Head from Vandals to Roaring Meg

13/20 Bates Motel/Solid Mandala
72m E3 (5b,6a,5b,5b) Torrans, Sheridan, 1980; Manson, Smith (first free ascent), 1981
Start: At the foot of the arête right of Aifric and left of the grassy gully leading to the big vegetated corner of ESP (4c).
1   24m Climb the left of three short overhanging grooves, to a short corner on the left. Up corner and step left on to arête. Continue up wall for 1m and traverse right (crux) to crack. Up crack to belay below pod.
2   24m Step down and across to arête and crack. Climb crack to foot of ramp and corner. Reach high hold on left wall and continue up ramp to ledge and belay.
3   12m Up layback crack above.
4   12m Gain huge flake and climb crack above.

13/21 Roaring Meg
100m VS (4c,4b,4c) Torrans, McGuinness, 1975
1   35m Climb the crack to overhang, which is climbed on the left by laybacking and bridging. Continue up crack to ledges and belay on flakes.
2   35m Climb crack to reach ramp on right. Easily up ramp to point where crack narrows and steepens; one awkward move to reach belay ledge.
3   30m Climb corner to long narrow shelf. Cross this and climb corner with care.

13/22 Cuchulainn
78m E2 (5a,5c,5c) Torrans, Sheridan, 1977
Start: Route takes the groove as described for Roaring Meg. Shares first belay with Roaring Meg, but continues straight up the wall.
1   33m Climb the crack until a move left on to small ledges. Move up and back into crack (difficult). Continue up crack passing some old rotting wedges (sustained) to reach a recess and short off-width crack. Gain the sloping ledge above. Continue up crack to belay on large flakes as for Roaring Meg.

The main wall of Fair Head from Conchubair to Salango

2   21m Gain the ramp above the belay, then move back left into corner and crack with a flake at bottom right. Climb crack to overhang, move out left over this to reach a small shelf on good but sustained jamming. Climb a few feet to reach a thin crack with groove on the right. Bridge up crack and groove to reach overhang. Climb this on good jams to reach yet another small shelf. Up 1m to small belay below undercut off-width crack.

3   24m Climb off-width — jam or layback up to jammed block (strenuous). Continue up with increasing difficulty to ledge at foot of grassy groove. Up this to belay.

13/23 Conchubair
60m E2 (5a,5c) Higgs, Ryan, 1980
This route takes the large open-book corner approximately 90m right of the huge boulder.
Start: By scrambling up to base of corner from the left — belay. The first ascenders took a hanging belay at the top of the corner, but it is now considered safer to belay on the ledge at 27m, as described below.

1   27m Climb the corner crack to ledge on left wall and belay.

2   33m Continue up the corner with increasing difficulty, passing bulges, to resting place near top of corner (peg *in situ*). Move left on good foothold to thin crack. Gain crack and climb steeply to the overhang (crux). Climb this on good layaway holds to reach into V-chimney. Up this, exiting left near top.

13/24 Blind Pew
60m E2 (5a,5b) Higgs, Goulding, 1978
Start: Approximately 20m to the right of Conchubair there is a mass of overhangs about three-quarters of the way up the cliff. Blind Pew takes the first corner to the right of these.

1   24m Climb the corner for 4m, then traverse left (or continue straight up the corner at 5b) and gain the obvious groove. Up this on good holds to off-width crack. Climb this with difficulty to a good ledge.

Roaring Meg, Tom Hand on the crux moves of Pitch 1

2   **36m** Climb the slightly overhanging corner above the ledge
(good holds on left wall after 9m) and continue up a delicate scoop
to the base of two grooves. Step across into right-hand groove and
move up into corner. Climb the corner crack with increasing
difficulty to the top. Block belay.

13/25 Mizzen Star
60m E2 (5b,5b) Torrans, Sheridan, 1977
Start: At the foot of the arête left of a vegetated
chimney-cum-corner and immediately right of Blind Pew.
1   **39m** From the bottom of the arête, climb the short groove and
crack to reach a light-brown flake. Hard move up flake to reach
good jugs. Move right to base of crack. Sustained jamming up crack
to overhang. Climb this to good jug on the right. Continue up crack
with difficulty to reach narrow ledge. Move left to good belay.
2   **21m** Climb the wall behind the belay to a ledge. Move right
and climb the wall on side pulls and bridging to reach a thin crack. A
long reach and a difficult mantelshelf to reach groove, then up this
to overhang with chockstone. Up past the overhang on left to crack,
which is followed to easy but doubtful-looking rock.

13/26 Titanic
63m E2 (5b,5c) Higgs, Ryan (two aid points), 1977; Livesey,
Torrans (first free ascent), 1977
Start: This route takes the first clean groove right of Mizzen Star,
10m left of Salango, with an overhang at half-height.
1   **21m** Climb the deep groove — delicate moves at 8m. Continue
up over a small bulge and then more easily to a steep finger crack.
Climb this to ledge out on the left.
2   **42m** Step back right and climb the steep crack to a resting
place below the overhang. Climb this (crux) and gain a sharp crack.
Climb the crack to a ledge, continue to a rocking chockstone from
where difficult climbing leads to good footholds on the left.
Continue over bulge on good hold to ledge. Finish up a short steep
crack.

Mizzen Star, Calvin Torrans on the crux moves around the overhang
on the first pitch

13/27 Salango
60m E3 (5b,5c) Torrans, Sheridan, Tasker (two aid points), 1976;
Livesey, Higgs (first free ascent), 1977
Route takes the cracked arête 16m left of Equinox.
Start: From top of a large boulder which forms cave.

1   36m Easy climbing up groove to awkward step. Up left to
reach a sloping ledge overhang which is climbed on good jams to
reach a finger-jamming crack. Up this with difficulty to belay under
overhang.

2   24m Climb the overhang (difficult) to reach the steep
strenuous crack above. Up this (crux) to a groove which is followed
to an overhanging flake. A difficult and sensational layaway over
overhang, to reach good jugs and top.

13/28 Equinox
60m E2 (5b,5b) McHugh, Billane (two aid points), 1974; Torrans,
Sheridan (first free ascent), 1977
Start: Takes the big steep corner left of the overhanging wall
containing Wall of Prey — i.e., the first corner on the
seaward-facing part of the crag left of the Ballycastle descent gully.

1   39m Climb the corner to overhang with sustained bridging and
jamming, slightly harder at the black crack at 12m. Climb the
overhang to small stance and belay.

2   21m Continue up the corner crux to overhang. Sensational
moves over the overhang lead to a ledge. Easier ground to top.

13/29 Wall of Prey
75m E4 (6a,5c) Strapcans, Jenkin, 1979
Start: This route takes an impressive line up the huge wall on the
left-hand (eastern) side of the Ballycastle descent gully, left of
Hell's Kitchen, passing the overhangs on the right.

The left wall of the Ballycastle descent gully (B.D.G.): b marks the belay
ledge shared by 13/33 and 13/34

1   36m Climb the groove on the left until it is possible to gain a thin crack in the right arête leading to the 'Hanging Fangs'. Place a peg runner on the right and begin a series of committing moves into the groove below the upper overhang. Follow the thin crack to flake belays on Green Slab. Foothold stance.

2   39m Climb the right-hand crack, stepping into the left one for a few moves until you are forced back right. Climb the bulge above until sloping holds give access to top.

13/30 Hell's Kitchen
66m HVS (5a,5a) McKenzie, Richardson, 1974
Start: The bottom left of the Ballycastle descent gully has a narrow wall containing four grooves. This route takes the largest of these, forming the corner boundary between the wall containing Wall of Prey and this narrow wall.

1   36m Climb ramp to groove which is gained by climbing wall on the left (difficult). Enter the groove and climb to belay flake on the left.

2   30m Continue up the groove until delicate step up (crux) can be made to good finishing hold on the right.

13/31 Ocean Boulevard
60m E3 (5c,5b) Torrans, Irving, 1978
Start: The groove right of Hell's Kitchen is Manannan, E1. Immediately right of this is a small grassy bay from which two routes run up. Ocean Boulevard takes the groove on the left.

1   39m Climb groove for 2m until a move left to a flake on the wall leads to a large ledge. Continue up slanting crack on the right to overhang below groove and thin crack. Climb this with increasing difficulty to a small ledge and belay.

2   21m Climb the crack and overhanging rock above the belay to a hanging nose of rock. Move right to a light-coloured ledge at foot of a crack. Up this (difficult) to small ledge. Move left to corner which is followed to an overhang. Step right to edge of crack and blocks to the top.

Girona, Robert Lawson stepping off the pinnacle at the start of the second pitch

13/32 Aoife
57m E1 (5b,5a) Torrans, Sheridan, 1976
Start: The groove line right of Ocean Boulevard in the grassy bay.
1   32m Climb the groove to steep corner under overhanging flakes. Layback around these to gain a resting place on the top flake. Continue up a short groove which tapers into a crack. Climb the crack on good jams and jammed flakes with increasing difficulty to good ledge and belay.
2   25m Climb the wall behind belay for 2m. Move right up a short ramp to a corner. A hard move up the corner leads to a good jam behind a flake. Continue up the corner for 1m where a move left can be made to reach a flake. One awkward move up the crack above the flake leads to easy ground.

13/33 Girona
63m VS (4c,4c) Billane, Torrane, 1976
This route, one of the best on the crag for the grade, takes a crack line on the left wall of the Ballycastle descent gully, just right of the series of corners containing the previous three routes.
Start: Under the large pinnacle of rock, visible from the top of the gully, in a small groove blocked by an overhang at 8m.
1   43m Climb the groove to the overhang, which is overcome using good bridging holds on the right and a hard move back into the crack above (crux). Continue up the crack trending slightly right then back left to a large ledge right of the huge pinnacle.
2   20m Chimney up behind and surmount the pinnacle. Step on to the wall above and climb a series of awkward mantelshelves to the top.

13/34 Chieftain
70m VS (4b,4b) Torrans, Mitchell, 1974
Start: Takes a deep, rightward-slanting V-groove, just right of Girona.
1   43m Climb the groove for 4m. Then either continue up the groove or move right on to the arête. A thin move on the arête leads to good jugs also reached by continuing up the groove to step delicately left below a small overhang. Continue up the arête before moving left to a good ledge as for Girona.

2   27m Up the crack immediately above the belay to the foot of the deep groove. Enter the groove on good jugs and follow this more easily to the top.

13/35 Eithne Inguba
72m E1 (5b,4c) Sheridan, Torrans, 1978
Start: The buttress to the right (west) of the Ballycastle descent gully is split by a wide groove. Eithne Inguba takes the first clean corner right of this, about 45m from the bottom of the gully.

1   45m Up overhanging block to bottom of a corner below a small bulge. Step left and climb wall for about 2m until you can move back into the corner, which is followed to a small overhang. Move left and up for 2m before traversing left below a bulge. Move back right and up small ledges to reach a steep crack on right leading to an overhang. Climb the crack and make a high step on to a slab on the left, using an undercut crack to reach hand jam (crux). Easier climbing leads to blocky ledges.

2   27m From blocks climb steep cracks trending leftwards up wall above to reach vegetated ledge. Continue straight up for 2m, move around left into corner and up cracks to short groove and overhang, which is climbed on the right.

13/36 Argosy
69m E1 (5a,4b) Higgs, Somers, 1978
Start: As for Eithne Inguba, below hanging block.

1   48m Climb short wall, passing dubious hanging block on left side, and gain ledges above. Move diagonally right to short wall below corner groove. Climb wall on widely-spaced holds (crux) and gain the bottom of corner. Up this, using sharp corner crack and good holds on the left wall. At small overhang step left and gain a narrow ramp. Climb ramp (delicate to start) to reach good ledges leading left. Move up behind blocks to belay.

2   21m Move up the blocky crack just left of the large spike and continue up weakness to a stance below a wide crack. Climb crack to grassy niche above; up pointed block on the left and step across right to reach a big hold. Finish up short groove to top. Nut belay on right.

13/37 Odyssey

66m VS (4c,4a,4b) Higgs, Hand, 1978

Start: This route takes the corner with square-cut overhangs just right of Argosy.

1   22m Move up small ledges then climb leftwards via a small overlap to gain a sloping ledge below the corner. Climb the corner (high step to start) and just below the overhang step out left to a large ledge on the arête. Climb short wall to a good stance and nut belay.

2   23m Climb directly above belay to thin crack. Pass under this on left to a fine position on the arête. Follow this and the groove above to a grassy platform and block belay.

3   21m Finish up Pitch 2 of Argosy.

13/38 Dearg Doom

69m VS (4b,4c,4c) Howard, Kerr, 1977

Start: Route takes a corner crack 2m right of Odyssey.

1   23m Climb the wide crack using good holds on the left wall to gain a large ledge 6m below an overhang.

2   25m Ascend groove to left end of the overhang, move right around and under overhang (crux), and enter crack behind flake. One awkward move leads to easier jamming. Mantelshelf on to large platform, step right on to block, step left again and up, then back right to enter a groove which leads to a large terrace.

3   21m Easily up vegetation and flakes to base of weakness. Climb for 6m on jugs to enter chimney, turning dubious block on the right. Strenuous moves lead to a step left on to block. Up twin cracks to the top.

The next set of routes is described in relation to The Prow — the obvious undercut buttress to the right of Dearg Doom.

The wall to the right of the Ballycastle descent gully: b marks belay ledge

13/39 Pyrrhic Victory

66m E1 (5a,5b) Lawson, Stelfox, 1980

Start: About 30m left of The Prow — immediately left of the undercut band of rock.

1   27m Climb easily up corner groove to the jammed block at 24m. Traverse right across the slab (crux) to belay ledge.

2   39m Climb the twin cracks above — sustained and strenuous. Difficulties ease slightly above the mid-way bulge.

13/40 Black Taxi

42m E1 (5b) Torrans, Sheridan, 1976

Start: The first crack right of The Prow is Wagger Moon, E1 (5c), followed by The Doffer, E1 (5b), which shares the same start. Black Taxi takes the crack immediately right of The Doffer, starting at the foot of a deep groove. Climb vegetated groove right of shallow groove for about 1m. Delicately step left on to a good ledge on slabby wall, climb up and slightly left, then back right to good ledge on good flat jugs, widely spaced. Climb up into crack, continue up this on good jams (difficult in places) to large rocking block jammed in crack. Up over block to jammed flake. Climb crack, using jammed flakes (crux) and continue over final small bulge to the top.

13/41 Mongrel Fox

42m E1 (5b) Torrans, Sheridan, 1977

Start: This route takes the wide twin cracks just right of Black Taxi on the undercut prow, and starts up a deep groove right of the Black Taxi slab. Climb groove to overhang at 10m. Climb the overhang on the left and gain a small niche. Jam up twin cracks and stand on block. Continue up twin cracks on the right to reach good ledges. Continue up right-hand crack by bridging and jamming, until it is possible to move left into base of scoop (resting place). Step back right into crack with difficult climbing to reach jammed blocks and top.

Odyssey, Ken Higgs on the first ascent. Dearg Doom takes the deep crack to the right

13/42 Thunderhips
39m E1 (5b) Torrans, Billane, 1975
Start: Immediately right and round the corner from Mongrel Fox, a corner runs down from the top, tapering out about 7m from the ground. Thunderhips is climbed by moving left into this corner after climbing the crack to right to start— Fireball. Climb the initial crack of Fireball for 7m to small foothold on the left wall. Traverse left to a good crack which is followed to a depression. Climb blocks and continue up crack with increasing difficulty.

13/43 Fireball
39m E1 (5b) Ryan, Higgs, 1976
Start: As for Thunderhips. Climb the crack, but where Thunderhips traverses left at 7m continue on sustained good hand jams until large holds on the left can be reached and used to gain a deep groove. Climb the groove with a difficult bulge near the top.

13/44 Midnight Cruiser
36m E1 (5b) Ryan, Nugent, 1979
Start: Just right of Fireball take the deep groove-cum-crack, finishing up twin cracks. Climb up to the overhang at 6m. Surmount this, using a flake on the left wall, and continue up to resting footholds on the right wall at mid-height. Continue up twin cracks (crux) with a difficult finish on flat holds.

13/45 Communication Breakdown
36m E1 (5b) Higgs, O'Brien, 1979
Takes a diagonal line up wall between Midnight Cruiser and Railroad.
Start: A few feet right of Midnight Cruiser below a short wide crack. Up wide crack and climb groove above mainly on the left wall. At 18m step right and pull into the steep groove on the right. A couple of thin moves up this lead to good holds on the right. Follow these up to overhang on Railroad. Climb overhang and crack above to top.

The Prow

13/46 Railroad
36m E1 (5b) Higgs, Ryan, 1977
Start: 9m to the right of Fireball there is a square-cut overhang with a martin's nest. This route starts below a flaky wall just left of this overhang. Climb the flaky wall (delicate) to a horizontal break at 7m. Move up crack on the right and continue with sustained difficulty up twin cracks. Avoid a very loose rightward possibility near the top of the cracks, and climb directly up to the overhang. Take this on good holds and jams, finishing up a steep crack to the top.

13/47 Sabre Rattler
38m HVS (4c) Torrans, Sheridan, 1980
Start: The corner crack right of Railroad is Balooba, VS (4b). Sabre Rattler takes the arête right of Balooba. Climb arête — nut runner at 12m in crack on left of arête. Up over short bulge to short crack, which is followed to platform. Up chimney on right to platform and up the thin crack above (difficult).

Right of Sabre Rattler is a buttress of rock undercut by a short overhang near its base. Contractions, VS (4c), climbs this overhang and the cracked wall above.

13/48 Fath mo Bhuartha
24m HVS (5b) Somers, Dwyer, 1977
Start: Beyond the undercut buttress containing Contractions is an inset wall split by many cracks. In the left corner is Good Morning Judge, HVS (5a). Fath mo Bhuartha starts about 1m right of the sapling at the foot of Good Morning Judge. Climb a slightly rightward-trending crack for 6m to good ledge. Using both cracks, proceed with difficulty past two bulges and move up right-hand crack. Continue straight up final bulge using poor finger jams (crux).

The Fence, Ian Rea climbing. The deep crack of The Black Thief is to his left and the (now cleaned) cracks of The Offence to his right

13/49 GBH
24m E3 (6a/b) Torrans, Sheridan, (one aid point) 1979; Murphy, ni Chiosain (first free ascent), 1982
Start: Takes the crack immediately right of Fath mo Bhuartha. Up the deep crack on excellent jams to the bulging wall. Climb this on well-spaced flat holds to gain a small rounded foothold. Difficult climbing up the thin crack with poor finger slots and a high step to reach a sloping foothold and the crux moves.

13/50 The Black Thief
24m VS (4b) Torrans, Sheridan, 1976
Start: Takes crack right of GBH. Up blocky ledges and the groove above on flat holds and jams, using the left-hand crack for about 7m. Move left on to the obvious block ledge, up the centre of the wall above, and then back into the right-hand crack to exit.

13/51 The Fence
24m VS (4c) Torrans, Billane, 1976
Start: Takes the first crack and groove right of The Black Thief. Climb groove using crack and footholds on left wall. Climb overhang on good jams and continue up crack to the top.

13/52 The Offence
24m HVS (5a) Stelfox, Lawson, 1980
Start: Just right of The Fence. Climb up on arête using blocks on the right. Continue up the arête to the base of cracks on right-hand side of the arête. Climb cracks (crux) to ledge on right. Continue up crack to top of large pillar on the left. Step back into crack and continue to the top.

14 Ballygalley Head, Antrim
GR 382080 Sheet 9, 1:50,000

Introduction A volcanic intrusion composed of dark columnar
dolerite. Easy access and high quality make it a popular crag for
local climbers — almost a mini Fair Head! Most routes follow
excellent jamming cracks in sound dolerite. About 40 routes at
present, mostly around 25m to 30m in height.

The crag is generally considered in three sections: on the left
above the layby is the Stable Gully area; in the middle is the
Roadside Wall and on the right the Castle Gully area. The greatest
concentration of good routes is in this latter area. Needless to say,
climbing beside the road requires extreme caution, and care should
also be taken not to disrupt traffic.

Access The crag is situated on the A2 Antrim coast road,
immediately south of Ballygalley village. Cars can be left at the
quarry entrance, about 100m south of the crag. Although some
routes have been climbed in the quarry, they are generally of poor
quality, and a voluntary ban on climbing is observed to protect the
nesting seabirds.

Accommodation The roadside nature of the crag prevents any
camping in the immediate vicinity. There is, however, a youth hostel
in Ballygalley village a few hundred metres from the crag.

Stable Gully area

14/1 Iky-Mo
15m S (3c) Agnew, Smyth, 1967
Start: Second crack system from left end of crag. Bridge up the twin
cracks, pulling over left at mid-height. Continue up and right to a
small ledge. Finish up either crack, left-hand one being harder.

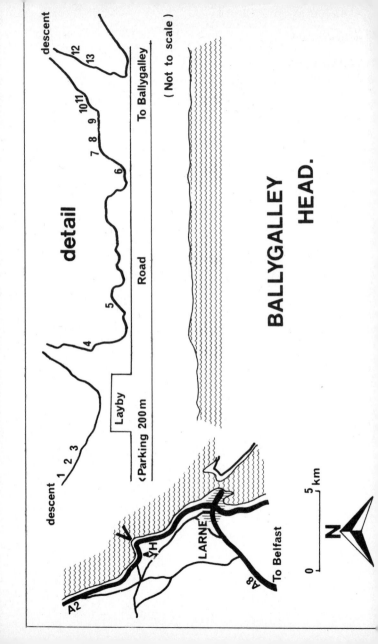

descent

1 2 3

detail

4

5

6

7 8 9 10 11

12
13

descent

Layby

< Parking 200 m

Road

To Ballygalley

(Not to scale)

A2

YH

LARNE

A8   To Belfast

BALLYGALLEY
HEAD.

N

0   5 km

14/2 Lucky Strike
28m HVS (5a) Cowan, 1968
Start: The thin crack about 3m right and below Iky-Mo. The route
follows the crack directly — the crux being a series of delicate
layback moves just below mid-height.

14/3 Reprisal
28m VS (4b) McGrath, Agnew, 1968
Start: The crack about 1m right of Lucky Strike. Using the crack
and the right-hand wall gain a small foothold on the right. From
here climb up the crack over a little notch (crux) to a large ledge.
Easier climbing to the top.

14/4 American Beauty
30m VD Rea, Maguire, Lindsay, 1980
Start: The large open-book corner at the foot of Stable Gully. The
corner crack system is climbed on a glut of holds directly to the top.
Excellent for the grade.

Roadside Wall area

14/5 Dirty Sox
33m VS (4b) Price, Murray, 1979
Start: From the grassy bay about 5m to the right of Stable Gully.
Climb the crack rising from the back of this bay on the left. The
obvious bulge at about 10m provides the crux. From here follow the
crack to a good ledge, moving left over overhanging rock to the
finish.
   The crack immediately to the right is Silent Running, HS, which
suffers from the lack of a good top belay.

Castle Gully area

14/6 Vindication
30m HVS (5b) Agnew, McCartney, 1968
Start: On the road at the bottom of the buttress forming the
left-hand end of the bay. The route follows the crack up the
right-hand side of the buttress. Climb the crack awkwardly for 12m
to a small grass ledge. Move on up by jamming or wide bridging. It
is possible to move out left on to the arête (Dire Straits, E3, 5c) for
a rest, but it proves difficult to regain the crack. As the groove
steepens better holds materialise and the top section is best climbed
facing left.

14/7 Cat's Eyes
30m VS (4c) Griffin, 1972
Start: In a shallow recess 1m right of Vindication. Climb the corner
crack until the angle eases. Move delicately up and right across the
wall to gain a parallel crack that runs down from the top overhang.
This is followed with one awkward move to the top.
    The next thin crack to the right is taken by Nightflight, E1 (5b),
then comes:

14/8 Deadline
30m HVS (5a) Lawson, Stelfox, 1979
Start: The thin crack about mid-way between Cat's Eyes and
Kleptomaniac. The crack is followed more or less directly to the
top. The crux is in the lower section, gaining the obvious small ledge
at mid-height but the route is sustained in difficulty.

Ballygalley Head, with Stable Gully in the foreground, the Roadside
Wall in the centre, and the mouth of Castle Gully just before the corner
arête

14/9 Kleptomaniac
30m VS (4c) Crymble, Beattie, 1968
Start: Right-hand of the first short road-facing wall, mid-way
between Vindication and Castle Gully. The route takes the obvious
wide crack straight up the wall, the crux being the bulge about
two-thirds height.

14/10 Star Spangled Banner
25m HVS (4c/5a) Griffin, 1971
Start: Below the overhanging corner, just right of Kleptomaniac,
facing across the Gully. Up over the first overhang to gain the
corner crack (strenuous). Follow the corner on small holds with
increasing difficulty, finally pulling out to the top of a pillar on the
left to finish.

14/11 Clearway
25m E1 (5b) Stelfox, Lawson, 1979
Start: About 1m right of Star Spangled Banner following the
rightward-trending crack line. Up over the initial overhang to a
good ledge at 3m. From here a series of strenuous but well
protected layback moves leads to a small niche about 3m below the
top. One more awkward move leads to easier ground.

14/12 Harry
25m VS (4c) Mills, Merrick (one aid point), 1978; McQuoid,
Bankhead, Stevenson (first free ascent), 1978
Start: This route takes the left-hand of two parallel,
leftward-trending cracks, about halfway down the right-hand wall of
Castle Gully. Beginning easily, follow the crack directly. Difficulties
increase, the crux being surmounting a short off-width section near
the top.

Left wall of Castle Gully: Vindication and Cat's Eyes being climbed by
Ken Higgs and Emmet Goulding respectively

14/13 Debbie

27m VS (4c) McQuoid, Merrick, 1978
Start: Takes the right-hand of the two cracks on the right Gully wall.
Follow the crack easily to the overhang at 5m. Climb this directly
and continue up the corner, fairly sustained, to the top.

Harry and Debbie on the right wall of the Castle Gully. The climber is
Alister McQuoid

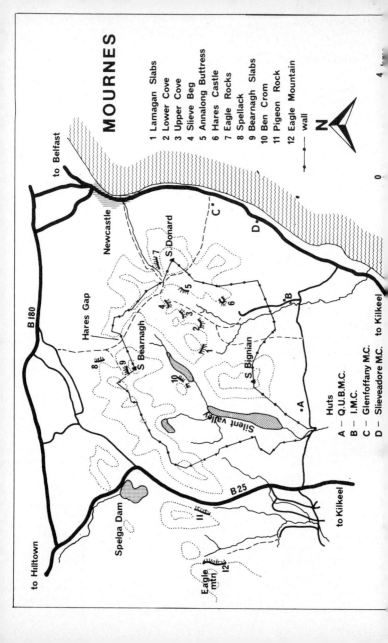

MOURNES

1 Lamagan Slabs
2 Lower Cove
3 Upper Cove
4 Slieve Beg
5 Annalong Buttress
6 Hares Castle
7 Eagle Rocks
8 Spellack
9 Bearnagh Slabs
10 Ben Crom
11 Pigeon Rock
12 Eagle Mountain
— wall

N

Huts
A — Q.U.B.M.C.
B — I.M.C.
C — Glenfoffany M.C.
D — Slieveadore M.C.

to Belfast

Newcastle

Hares Gap

Spelga Dam

to Hilltown

B 180

B 25

to Kilkeel

Silent valley

S. Donard

S. Bearnagh

S. Bignian

Eagle mtn.

Introduction to the Mourne Mountains, Co. Down

'Mourne Country' map, 1:25,000

The Mourne Mountains are a compact and picturesque range offering some splendid hill walking and rock climbing. They are situated about 48 km south of Belfast but, although the area is well supplied by roads on all sides, most crags have substantials walk-ins and a mountain atmosphere. Throughout the range, granite tors and faces emerge to provide some excellent and varied climbing. The rock is generally sound, of a compact nature and usually rounded, forcing reliance on the excellent friction. Protection is often sparse or difficult to arrange, although Friends have made dramatic changes to the seriousness of some routes.

The exposed tors of Slieve Binnian, Slieve Bernagh and Hen Mountain provide some excellent short routes — almost of a problem nature. They contain the most rounded and weathered rock with minimal protection. The easy-angled slabs of Slieve Bernagh and Slieve Lamagan give routes up to 150m long, rarely exceeding S in difficulty. The steeper faces of Slieve Beg, Spellack, Eagle Mountain and Cove Mountain give many excellent routes, mainly in the upper grades, whilst the outcrops of Eagle Rocks, Annalong Buttress and Hare's Castle provide good routes of all grades.

With over 400 routes on around 20 crags to choose from, it proved impossible to include all of the classic climbs. Instead, to do full justice to those crags offering the most concentrated quality, a selection not only of routes but of crags as well has been made. Reference should be made to the local guide for more detailed information.

Access The crags are widely scattered throughout the area and access is usually possible from a number of directions. Approaches are described under each crag section.

Accommodation Although Newcastle is the climbing centre, accommodation is widespread. There are youth hostels at Kinnahala as well as at Newcastle. There are also four

Mountaineering Club Huts which can be used by the visitor with the approval of the owner club (See p. 20 for addresses). In addition there are usually excellent camping sites to be found below the crags.

The Annalong Valley Crags

The Annalong Valley is one of the most picturesque and accessible valleys of the Mournes. It is best entered from the south — by Rourkes Park (358223) or the Carrick Little Track (345219). Guarded on all sides by crags, the valley provides a good concentration of quality climbing. To the west lies the summit of Slieve Binnian, whose spine of tors provides short problems of all grades and whose slopes are liberally sprinkled with outcrops, mainly however, grassy and undeveloped. Further up on the same side is Slieve Lamagan (331255) which presents long easy slab routes on its southern side. Difficulties above S are hard to find — endless combinations and variations are possible. The classic route is FM, 154m, VD, which takes the central line, passing the step by the obvious break at mid-height. The first major crag of the valley is on the next mountain to the north — Cove Mountain.

Lower Cove, with the four corners marked

15 Lower Cove, Mourne Mts
GR 337260

Set about half-way up the valley, about an hour's walk from the
Carrick Little Track start, these cliffs, although unimpressive from a
distance, are among the steepest and best in the Mournes.
South-facing and largely free of vegetation, they dry quickly. Four
large corners conveniently divide up the cliff — they are numbered
from left to right.

15/1 First Corner
27m HS (4b) Devlin, McGrath, 1965
Start: At the left-hand end of the crag a short boulder-filled gully
borders on the left the sharp edge of the First Corner, taken by the
route of the same name. Up the edge to a ledge on the left.
Continue straight up the edge (crux) or more easily up the gully wall
directly above.

15/2 Dot's Delight
39m HVS (4c) Kavanagh, Devlin, 1964
A classic climb offering a demanding and steady lead.
Start: 10m right of First Corner below a series of overhanging
flakes. Follow a slight depression in the wall diagonally right to a
small ledge at half-height. Move left (peg runner) and then up to
gain a thin traverse line (crux). Follow this to a large ledge and
continue up the easier wall above.

15/3 Gynocrat
30m HVS (5a) Stelfox, McQuoid, 1980
Start: The gully wall left of the Second Corner and Aristocrat is split
by a deep crack, starting 5m up the wall. Climb the wall right of the
crack, and via a series of difficult moves surmount the overhang and
gain a ledge at the foot of the crack. Ascend the crack and wall more
easily to a good ledge. A difficult move off the ledge (crux) leads to
easier ground with a step right below the impending head wall to
finish. Mild in the grade.

First Corner, Ian Rea on the final arête

15/4 Aristocrat

35m HVS (5a) McQuoid, Currans, 1980

Start: Takes a line up the Second Corner, starting 4m up on the left-hand wall. Move up and begin a delicate traverse right across a line of small holds and undercut flakes, to reach a groove line near the corner edge. Climb this with difficulty, past a good ledge on the right (possible belay) and on to the steep wall above. A further difficult move leads to the easier but unprotected wall above. Friends are useful for protection. High in the grade.

15/5 Pillar Variant

40m S (4a,3c) Moorhead, Stead (Pitch 1), 1967; Gribbon, Boyd, White (Pitch 2), 1956

An interesting route starting on the pillar of rock on the left-hand side of the Third Corner and finishing up the edge of the corner itself.

Start: In a grassy recess below a dirty, overhanging crack, left of the clean pillar of rock.

1   25m Move right across broken ground on to the pillar, or climb the steep wall below by a rounded layback edge (5a). Ascend the steep face of the pillar on good holds at first, becoming smaller as one nears the top. Belay on blocks above the deep chimney of Third Corner, S.

2   15m Delicate footwork up the edge above leads to the top. A harder variation (4c) can be followed by making a gymnastic move left to gain the sloping crack leading to the top.

Dot's Delight, with climber on the crux traverse. First Corner is the arête on the left skyline

15/6 Brewer's Gloom
45m S (3c,3c,3c) Grindley and party, 1961
Start: In a recess right of the Fourth Corner.
1   **18m** Up the well-cracked wall on the right and move right around the corner to a small diedre. Ascend this awkwardly and move right to belay.
2   **12m** Mantelshelf awkwardly and traverse right around an airy corner to belay.
3   **15m** Climb the steep wall above on good holds, moving left towards the top.

15/7 Praxis Direct
43m HVS (5b,3c) Ingrim, Shelly (first ascent), 1961; Smith, Cole (direct start), 1978
Start: 10m right of Brewer's Gloom in a 'Gothic' recess in the middle of a light-coloured area of rock.
1   **28m** Bridge up the recess to gain the steep crack. Follow this with increasing difficulty to enter a chimney at half-height. Continue up and belay below the final pitch of Brewer's Gloom.
2   **15m** As for Brewer's Gloom.

15/8 Les Jeune Filles
30m E1 (5a/b) Currans, McQuoid, 1980
A strenuous and sustained route in a superb situation, though not technically demanding for the grade.
Start: At the left end of the wall. Move up and right fairly easily but strenuously to a ledge and peg at 15m. From here move up and left to the ledge below the obvious overhang. Finish by this, starting from the left-hand side of the ledge.

Praxis Direct, Martin Manson moving out of the initial recess

16 Slieve Beg, Mourne Mts
GR 340275

One of the best and most impressive of the Mourne crags, Slieve Beg lies in a commanding position at the head of the Annalong Valley. The most obvious feature is the huge central gully — the Devil's Coach Road. To the left is the main face, south-east-facing and characterised by a series of corners, and to the left again are two large, south-facing areas separated by a steep grassy section. To the right of the Devil's Coach Road are more broken crags — the most obvious feature being a steep broad slab of rock taken by Mourne Maggie.

The crag can be reached either from the valley floor or from Newcastle via the Glen River, over the Slieve Commedagh/Slieve Donard col and then west along the Brandy Pad, in about 1½ hours. Routes are described from left to right, looking from the valley floor.

16/1 Devil's Rib
54m VD Johnston, Gault, Archer, 1947
Start: At the left-hand end of the south-facing walls, just right of a series of scree gullies and more broken rock, is a prominent rib of rock. Start at the base of this.
1   **20m** Climb from the base of the rib to a belay on the right.
2   **34m** Wind up the rib to a selection of finishes. Impressive situations at a reasonable grade.

Slieve Beg from the Annalong Valley, with the arrow of scree pointing up the Devil's Coach Road (D). M marks the main face; r, the Devil's Rib; and m, Mourne Maggie

16/2 Shadowfax

40m E1 (5b) Torrans, Bruce, (1 aid point) 1974; Stelfox, Lawson, (first free ascent) 1983

Start: Below twin cracks 16m right of Devil's Rib, reached by traversing right along a grassy rake running across the crag from the base of the rib. Climb the twin cracks, moving into the right-hand one as difficulties and angle increase. Follow this with sustained difficulty until a good hold gives access to ledges on the left. Follow cracks leading back right above, easily at first but harder as the rock steepens around the final overhangs. Good cracks lead through these to the top and block belay.

16/3 The Fiddler

97m HVS (4b,5b,4b) Torrans, Jenkins (three aid points), 1969; Torrans, Sheridan (first free ascent), 1979

Start: At the lowest point of rock at the left-hand end of the main face. The route takes a double diedre reached by a ramp running from right to left.

1   27m Move right to gain the upper ramp and climb the wide corner past two ledges to gain the belay ledge on the left below the double diedre, or more directly by the wall below the belay (5a).

2   30m Move right to a large block in the middle of the face. Up and left into diedre. Move up this, then right and strenuously up the overhanging wall above (crux). Move left and climb a short corner to belay on a pile of blocks.

3   40m Up the 12m cracked wall above, and scramble up heather and rock to belay.

The main face of Slieve Beg

16/4 Wabash Cannonball

80m VS (4c, 4a) Torrans, Billane, Baxter, 1974

Start: This route takes the left-hand of the huge diedres running the
full length of the main face, starting below and to the right.

1   37m Climb the crack for 7m and move left into corner. Ascend
this, easily at first, to a short steep diedre. Climb this directly or
swing left on to a large flake before moving back right to a large
block belay.

2   43m Up an awkward corner to reach the upper slab. This is
climbed via good cracks on the right to easier ground. A small arête
on the right provides a good finish (4b).

16/5 Satanic Majesty

*57m E2 (4c,5b) Crymble, Curran, Chambers, 1974; Torrans,
Billane (first free ascent), 1974*

The second huge diedre, 20m to the right of Wabash Cannonball,
gives one of the best routes of its grade in the Mournes.

Start: By scrambling up grass and rock to the foot of the groove.

1   15m Up groove and corner to ledge and peg belay.

2   42m Up wall to corner. Bridge around the small overhang
moving slightly right along obvious weakness. Move up and left
more easily, past sharp flakes and a good crack to below the
L-shaped overhang. Move right on to the wall below this and climb
up to a good ledge on the right (crux). Move back left and up easier
rock to finish.

Parallel Lines and Sweetie Mice. Dawson Stelfox is on the crux moves
of the first; Alan Currans bridges up the corner of Sweetie Mice just
before the move right on to the arête

16/6 The Devil's Alternative
68m E1 (5b,5a,4c) Stelfox, Maguire (Pitches 1 and 3), 1981;
Torrans (Pitch 2), 1976
This route takes a line across the wall right of Satanic Majesty, up a
corner crack shared with Shaughran, HVS (4c,5a,4a) and a steeply
overhanging corner to finish.
Start: Just right of Satanic Majesty — but best approached from the
right.

1   30m Up the short corner crack to a good ledge at the foot of
the
face. Up the corner ramp with increasing difficulty until a step left
can be made using a high hidden handhold to gain a V-groove on the
left (crux). Follow the obvious ramp line right, to a large block belay
at the foot of a corner, above another corner — that of Shaughran
(Pitch 1).

2   20m As for Shaughran. Climb the corner with increasing
difficulty to a wide crack leading back left. Up this on bridging holds
(crux) and poor jams to another block belay.

3   18m From here Shaughran takes the easy slabs to the right.
Much more interesting is the steep groove directly behind the
belay — moving left into the overhanging corner to finish on
massive holds.

The southern side of the Devil's Coach Road contains a number
of fine routes:

16/7 Polo
27m D Curran, Curran, 1972
Start: Just below the upper of two subsidiary gullies are four tall,
regular square-cut corners giving three routes all around VS. Just
right of these is a large corner taken by Polo.

At the lower end of the gully is a steep wall with an obvious
right-angled corner in the middle. The left arête of this wall is taken
by Tara's Halls, E1 (5b), whilst the corner contains Sweetie Mice.
The cracks in between are:

16/8 Parallel Lines

40m HVS (5a) Torrans, Sheridan, 1979

Up easily to a long ledge at 10m. Move left into parallel cracks (crux) which are followed with difficulty to a ledge. A steep broken wall leads to the top. Friends useful for protection.

16/9 Sweetie Mice

40m HVS (5a) McGuinness, Bruce, 1973

Climb the diedre, easily at first, but with increasing difficulty, just below the large sloping ledge. Continue up the corner, until at 25m, a bulge forces a dramatic move right on good holds to the edge. Continue up the edge to belay or step back left (5b) and continue up the corner.

16/10 Mourne Maggie

58m HVS (5a) Quinn, Holmes, 1977

Takes the obvious broad slab towards the right-hand end of the crag, with an overhang near the top.

Start: Under the overhanging right-hand side of the slab.

1   18m Climb a corner and move back on to a large ledge.

2   40m Up from left of ledge for 5m. Move right and up the diminishing crack system until a delicate move leads to a shallow scoop (crux). It is possible to belay here, but more satisfying to continue on to the top. Traverse left below the overhang to the obvious crack in its left-hand end. Ascend this on good holds to the top.

17 Annalong Buttress, Mourne Mts
GR 349272

This is a small but popular crag lying on the eastern side of the
Annalong Valley, just below the Slieve Donard/Chimney Rock
Mountain col. Access is either from the valley or via the Bloody
Bridge track from the Newcastle/Kilkeel Road (GR 388270)—
both about 1½ hours.

The crag is characterised by clean rock abounding in protrusions
and encrustations, but with a minimum of protection. Belays at the
top are often well back from the edge. The most obvious feature is
the deep corner (Hanging Corner, VD) at the left-hand end of a
steep wall which contains the finest routes.

17/1 Thin Crack
25m VS (4b/c) Earnshaw, Moore, 1964
The striking, straight, pockled crack just left of the centre of the
wall. The crux is low down and protection is available.

17/2 Warsaw Convention
27m VS (4b) Gribbon and party, 1962
The leftward-sloping crack, starting about 9m right of Thin Crack
and converging on it.

17/3 Spanish Flea
38m S (3c) Jenkins, Martin, Hedley, 1966
Start: At flakes on the wall right of Warsaw Convention, below an
obvious triangular block. Follow the flakes and the crack, pulling
right around the block to belay. Continue easily over the overhang
and crack above to an airy slab which is followed to the top, or move
left above the block following a further crack system to the slab.

17/4 Springtime
46m S (4a) Brown, Moore, 1964
Just right of Spanish Flea is a short steep crack which is followed to
the same triangular block as for Spanish Flea.

Thin Crack on the Annalong Buttress, Dawson Stelfox climbing

18 Hare's Castle, Mourne Mts
GR 345256

A prominent quarried knoll on the east side of the valley, near its mouth. Sound and clean rock gives excellent short routes of continuous interest. Access is easiest by following the Water Works road from Rourke's Park to the upper workings, marked by a crane boom. From here take a track up the right-hand side of the valley, finishing in a short steep climb up the side of a subsidiary stream to reach the quarry floor— about three-quarters of an hour. Descent is easiest by scrambling over the top and down the left-hand side.

At the left-hand side a huge boulder leans against the main crag. Block Route, D, climbs this and the easy cracks above.

18/1 Thin Arête
25m VS (5a) Devlin, Agnew, 1965
Start: This route follows the crest of the rib on the left of the face. After a difficult start (crux) move left and then right to gain a crack at 12m. Follow this to the top.

18/2 Third Party
25m VS (4c) Firth, Leeke, Wilkinson, 1960
Start: Climb the corner on the right of Thin Arête. The crux is the step left around the overhang, past an old aid peg.

18/3 Duet
25m VS (4b) Sloan, Milligan, 1960
Start: At the rib 10m right of Thin Arête. Climb the rib and move left to reach a short diedre. Move up and along the ledge, left, for 4m and surmount the overhanging wall to the top.

18/4 Hellfire Corner
22m HS (4b) Wilkinson, 1960
Start: At the right-hand end of the face. Gain a diedre from the right and by a series of strenuous but delicate moves gain a good ledge. Finish by a crack near the edge, passing a quarryman's feather.

Hare's Castle from the Quarry Platform

Trassey Valley Crags

Approached from the northern side of the Mournes, the Trassey
Valley provides access to two high-quality crags— the steep clean
walls of Spellack and the long slab routes of Bernagh Slabs. The tors
on the summit of Slieve Bernagh also provide a good range of
shorter routes.

Thin Arête. The square overhang of Third Party is in the top right of the
picture

19 Spellack, Mourne Mts
GR 313295

The Trassey Valley path, leading up to the prominent Hare's Gap, is reached by turning off the Bryansford/Hilltown road about 5 km from Bryansford and just after a right turn to Kilcoo as one leaves the forest edge. After passing over a small bridge, the road climbs steeply to a farm and parking place beside a gate. The track leads from here, through young forest, on to the open mountain, Spellack being the steep crag high on the right, on a spur of Slieve Meelmore. Follow the path until nearly opposite the crag, then cross the river and up steeply to its foot. Approximately 30 minutes from the road.

The main crag of Spellack is split by a grassy ramp into two tiers of steep clean rock, with more vegetated, easier angled crags to each side. At the left-hand end of the lower tier is a wide grassy gully, narrowing and steepening at the top to form Spellack Chimney, VD. Just right of this is:

19/1 White Walls
30m S (4a)
Start: This takes the obvious cracked white wall at the top of the crag and gives one of the best routes of its grade in the Mournes. Climb the slab below the wall by a series of grooves and small ledges. After reaching a large ledge on the right, step back left on to the steep wall. This is climbed directly, on excellent holds, in a very impressive situation.

The right-hand end of the lower main face presents a steep wall of rock containing:

Spellack: g marks the entrance to the gully leading up to Spellack Chimney and White Walls; a = approach ramp leading to start of 19/3 and 19/4, and descent from 19/2

19/2 Mad Dogs
35m E5 (6b) Douglas, Manson, (two aid points) 1980
Start: At the left end of the large grass ledge, part way up the
right-hand side of the face. Climb large flakes until level with the
first small overlap (jammed nut). Traverse left under this to
undercut holds below *in-situ* peg runner. Make difficult moves
straight up to peg (rest point). Climb overlap just left of peg to gain
ledge at base of inverted V. Step right to below peg (rest point).
Layback up right-hand side of inverted V, bridge out of top and step
right to reach side-pull above peg. Make a committing series of
moves (crux) up the featureless wall (no runners) to second inverted
V. From here, easier climbing leads to a small overhang. Swing out
left and up face to top. Good nut belay in square-cut corner.

   The upper tier, again a steep clean slab, contains a number of
fine, hard routes, of which the best are described below. A set of
Friends will be found essential for protection on most of the routes
on this wall.

19/3 Mirror Mirror
40m E3 (6a) Calow, Codling, Douglas, 1979
Start: Beneath a shield of downward-pointing flakes towards the
left-hand end of the wall. With difficulty climb over these flakes and
step right to a short horizontal crack. Continue directly up a shallow
groove (peg runner) to reach a long, wide, horizontal break.
Traverse right to a peg runner, step up and right, and then finish up
the prominent diagonal crack above.

Mad Dogs, Martin Manson on the first ascent

19/4 Warhorse

40m E4 (6a) Codling, Calow, Douglas, (one aid point) 1979
Start: Takes the waterworn wall mid-way between Mirror Mirror
and the fault at the right-hand end of the face (Cherub, HVS, 5a).
Follow a line of flakes diagonally right. Traverse right (peg runner)
and up to a thread. Up left to the first horizontal break using a poor
peg as a handhold. Make a long reach to gain a flat hold below the
second horizontal break. Using a pocket above this break, reach
high up left for a flake. Move right to reach another thread. This
thread was placed by abseil on the first ascent, but is not now *in situ*.
Extreme difficulty will be found in placing this whilst climbing.
Continue straight up to finish.

Warhorse, John Codling on the first ascent

20 Bernagh Slabs, Mourne Mts
GR 310283

Follow the Trassey path to where it forks below a large quarry.
Take the right-hand path leading up to the col between Slieve
Meelmore and Slieve Bernagh. The slabs are immediately to the left
of the col, which is marked by the striking Mourne Wall. About 1¼
hours from the road. Descent is made on the right, after crossing the
wall.

   The slabs offer long and relatively easy rock climbs on sound
granite.

20/1 Crooked Chimney
80m S (-,-,3c,4a,3c) Graham, Blakie, McMurray, 1949
Start: At the left-hand end of the slabs is a huge triangle of relatively
smooth slab. Crooked Chimney goes up this, continuing up the
obvious dog-leg chimney at the top of the slab. Start directly under
this.
1   **30m** Following a thin system of ribs leading up to the right
(either boldly on the left-hand edge or on the grass to the right)
reach a small ledge and spike belay.
2   **18m** Move up cracks and slabs on the right to a large grassy
ledge at the apex of the triangle.
3   **14m** Move left up a crack to the edge and follow the slabby
exposed rib back right.
4   **9m** Ascend with difficulty the off-width crack above (crux).
5   **9m** Finish by the dog-leg chimney or the deep crack on the
right.

20/2 Grand Central
91m VD
Start: 6m right of Crooked Chimney towards the right-hand edge of
the slab triangle directly below an overhang at the top of the route,
lying 12m right of the dog-leg chimney.
1   **34m** Up the slab to a stance at 17m. Follow the right-hand
groove to a belay.

Bernagh Slabs from approach track

2   **15m** Up, then traverse left, then up left again to the grass ledge as for Crooked Chimney Pitch 2.
3   **12m** Climb the tilted wall on the right and up to a triangular flake belay.
4   **12m** Move left up slab to rib edge and up to conical spike.
5   **18m** Follow the awkward chimney above to the top.
    One of the best routes on the crag is formed by combining Pitches 1 and 2 of Grand Central with Pitches 3 and 4 of Crooked Chimney.

20/3 Hypothesis
88m S (3c,4a,4a) Firth, Wilkinson, 1960
Start: 15m left of the shattered overlap wall which marks the right-hand edge of the slabs, below an obvious corner.
1   **34m** Easily up the slabs to the left-hand end of a short overlap curving down to the right. Up over this to large ledge and belay.
2   **34m** Move up, then follow the cracks diagonally left across the slab to the left-hand side of the short overlap above. Follow the adhesive cracks up the slab to another large ledge on the right.
3   **20m** Move left to a crack near the left edge and follow this to the top, or more easily straight up from the belay.

20/4 Crescent
88m VS (4a,4b,4a) Firth, Wilkinson, 1960
Start: This route takes the corners immediately to the right of Hypothesis, sharing belays and the top pitch. Pitch 2 is excellent when dry, but this takes a long period of good weather.
1   **34m** Starting at a small slab tongue, just to the right and above that of Hypothesis, move up to and along the base of the crescent-shaped overlap to its left-hand extremity, and join Hypothesis to the belay.
2   **34m** Straight up the corner above by wide bridging and good holds on the right-hand wall. Just before the top of the corner make a delicate move up and left to reach another groove running left to the left-hand edge of the overlap. Follow this and belay as for Hypothesis. Friends very useful for protection.
3   **20m** Continue to the top as for Hypothesis.

21 Pigeon Rock Mountain, Mourne Mts
GR 226236

These popular crags are found ten minutes' walk above the
Kilkeel/Hilltown road. The best climbing is on the large Left-Hand
Buttress and the south side of the small Right-Hand Buttress.

Left-Hand Buttress
Descend by a path down the left-hand side.

21/1 Virgo
90m VS (4a,4b,4b,4b) Moore, Porter, 1965
A tremendous route. The technical crux is considered to be on Pitch
2, but Pitch 3 provides the most demanding lead.
Start: The grass ledges at the base of the clean face on the
right-hand side of the crag end abruptly in a small grass ledge about
2m from the ground. Straight up from here the rightward-leaning
crack is B Special. Virgo moves up and traverses left under this,
then a long traverse back right again leads to the huge grass ledge
two-thirds of the way up the crag.
1   9m Climb twin cracks at the back of a small recess and squeeze
behind a huge triangular block to a chockstone belay.
2   21m Climb on to the sloping ledge above and up to the
overhanging block on the left. With difficulty move left and up off
the block, using a hidden hold on the left. Up the slab and two
mantelshelves to a belay at the far end of a rock ledge. An *in-situ*
peg belay can be found, above eye-level at the top of a flat block
above the middle of the belay ledge.
3   30m Move up and right on small holds to an awkward hold
mantelshelf. Continue moving right, up a short crack and then right
round the corner, and across the exposed traverse ending in a short
crack leading to the huge grass ledge.
4   30m Climb the diedre left of the nose and finish out left by two
mantelshelves.

21/2 B Special

72m E1 (4a,5c,4b) Cowan, Wray, 1969

1   **9m** As for Virgo.

2   **33m** Climb the overhanging block as for Virgo and continue up the overhanging wall to reach a pulpit. Continue up on to a steeply sloping ledge on the left. Step up and right on to good holds and move up to Virgo ledge.

3   **30m** Finish as for Virgo (Pitch 4).

21/3 Lunar Wall

73m HVS (5a,4b) Cowan, Torrans, 1968

Start: At the foot of the chimney, 4m right of Virgo.

1   **43m** Climb the chimney for 9m to a large loose block. Traverse left along steep wall for 5m into a groove. Up groove to reach a small triangular ledge. Go left up a series of ledges to the end of Pitch 3 of Virgo and the belay ledge.

2   **30m** As for Virgo Pitch 4.

21/4 Geraldine

69m E2 (4c,5c,4b) Torrans, Jenkins (VS + A2), 1977; Codling, Douglas (one aid point), 1979

Start: At the cracks on the face of the flat buttress of rock lying under two large overhangs 5m left of the gully that marks the right-hand end of the main rock face of the Left-Hand Buttress.

1   **12m** Climb the cracks to a ledge on the top of the buttress under the first overhang.

2   **27m** Surmount the first overhang with difficulty and continue more easily across the steep wall above. Difficulties increase to reach the *in-situ* bolt which gives access to a thin crack below and a good crack to the right of the large overhang. The crack relents after a few moves to lead left to Virgo ledge.

3   **30m** As for Virgo (Pitch 4), or from right of the large overhang on the nose to the right, make an ascending traverse of the wall to gain the arête and the top (5a).

Virgo, Alistair Acheson on the airy traverse of Pitch 3

Right-Hand Buttress

Descent is either by abseiling down Class Distinction (stake in place) or by continuing up the short rock pitches, S, above the stake to the top of the crag and walking right to the large gully at the right end of the crag.

21/5 Class Distinction

30m S (4a) Crymble and party, 1966

This excellent pitch takes the obvious open-book corner starting half-way up the crag.

Start: Just right of this at the base of a slabby wall. Climb up the left side of the wall, moving right, and then back left to the foot of the corner. Gain the undercut corner (crux) and ascend on bridging holds to the top.

21/6 Faerie Flight

27m S (4a) Moore, Porter, Browne, 1965

Start: 2m right of Class Distinction. Climb past a series of flakes to a clean slab on the right. Move delicately up and right across this to the steep wall above. Continue moving right to a short corner and the top.

21/7 Nuclear Wheelbarrow

30m HS (4b) Crymble, Plant

Start: 3m right of Faerie Flight there is a short wall with a huge grassy ledge on top. Above this are two prominent corners, the right-hand one of which contains a long clean overhang. Nuclear Wheelbarrow takes this corner. Ascend to the ledge and into the dark corner beyond. Bridge up and over the overhang, on to the slab above. Move up (crux) to gain excellent jugs, and step left into a short corner with a jammed block. Surmount this (awkward) and the corner above as for Faerie Flight.

Pigeon Rocks, Left-Hand Buttress: b marks the position of Virgo Ledge

Pigeon Rocks, Right-hand Buttress: a = the abseil stake at the top of Class Distinction (p. 242)

Class Distinction, Willie Brown-Kerr entering the final corner (p. 243)

21/8 Falcon

27m HS (4b,4a) Porter, Moore, 1965

Can be done in one pitch if the direct finish is being followed. The normal route presents considerable rope drag in this fashion.

Start: At bottom right of the wall are a pair of cracks and a niche forming a long inverted triangle of rock, 10m right of Class Distinction.

1   15m Climb the double cracks to the recess and exit by its left wall (crux). Move more easily up a broken wall, then step right to belay on top of a pillar.

2   12m Move up and right around the corner to finish up a groove leading back left or straight up the wall above the belay (4c). Up the ridge above to belay.

Falcon, Alan Currans climbing. The Direct Finish moves straight up from the block above and to his right; the normal route moves right around the arête to gain a steep slab

22 Eagle Mountain, Mourne Mts
GR 246224

Although the largest of the Mourne crags, the north-facing aspect generally restricts climbing to rare long periods of dry weather. In addition, a voluntary ban on climbing exists during the bird-nesting season of March to July. When conditions are good, however, there is excellent climbing in some very impressive situations.

The crag is reached by driving through Attical village, after turning off the Kilkeel/Hilltown road. After a sharp double turn over a bridge, turn right up a side road named Sandy Brae and continue past a Gaelic football pitch on to an untarred road to a river ford and farmhouse. Cars can be left just before the ford. Follow the track up the valley, keeping to the left-hand side, as the crag appears on the left. Continue up the main track past the crag, until a small track moving back left is encountered. Follow this to the base of the crag. About 1 hour from the ford.

The main features are the huge chimney at the left-hand end — Corpse Alley, VS, the impressive Great Corner on the middle of the main face, Great Gully — the obvious gully to the right — which is bounded in turn on the right-hand side by The Keep.

Descent is usually by Great Gully, an abseil peg being in place for the short rock step, VD, near the bottom.

22/1 Great Corner
94m HVS (4c,5a,4c,5a) Torrans, Jenkins, Merrick, 1967
Start: Below and to the left of the corner.
1 **18m** Climb cracks in the corner to the overhang. With difficulty move right around this and into the crack above. Move right over two ledges to peg belay.
2 **37m** Climb up and traverse delicately into the corner (crux). Move up cracks to the huge grass ledge in the middle of the corner.
3 **15m** Climb the parallel cracks in the steep slab above. Step left into a niche and up to a belay beneath the impending wall above.

Eagle Mountain. G marks the entrance to Great Gully; A, the Amphitheatre; and K, The Keep

4   24m Traverse left into the corner. Climb with difficulty the usually wet off-width cleft above.

22/2 Lassara Grooves
70m HVS (4c,5a) Curran, Henry, 1978; Stelfox, Ireland (first free ascent), 1980
Start: 30m right of Great Corner at a clean, straight diedre system.
1   30m From the blocks at the base of the corner groove, climb up and enter a chimney. Move up by bridging and chimneying until at 23m a step right can be made to a deep crack.
2   40m Climb the steep corner layback crack from the left side of the ledge to gain a triangular flake 4m up (crux). Easier climbing up grooves and corners leads to the top.

On the left-hand side of Great Gully, just to the left of the rock step, are two prominent overhang-capped grooves, both starting halfway up the crag. The left-hand of these is taken by Fool on a Hill, E2 (5c) and the right-hand one by Surplomb Sundae. Both can be reached by scrambling up a dirty gully leading left immediately above the rock step, or by Cretin's Groove, HS — the poor and crumbly crack line splitting the pillar of rock to the left of the rock step.

22/3 Surplomb Sundae
35m VS (4c) Kerr, Curran, 1976
A superb route, high in the grade, with incredible situations and considerable exposure.
Start: In the dark corner reached by scrambling up rocks and grass from the top of Cretin's Groove or the gully mentioned above. Climb the corner to the base of the bottomless chimney. With difficulty and trepidation, enter and climb this. Energetic moves over the capstone bring one to the final crack which is followed to the top.

Just to the right of Surplomb Sundae is *The Amphitheatre* — a bay of rock perched high above Great Gully. It is lined with short but generally good routes, the best being:

Lassara Grooves, Dawson Stelfox on the first pitch

22/4 Tullamona Cracks
35m VS (4c) Forsythe, Curran (one aid point), 1976; McClenaghan (first free ascent), 1981
Start: The series of cracks near the corner of the left-hand wall of The Amphitheatre. Climb the right-hand of two cracks with difficulty, until at 5m more generous holds appear. Steep but straightforward climbing leads past a rocking chockstone at 15m. At the top of the crack move right and finish up the slab.

On the Great Gully side of The Keep, near the upper end, is the obvious slanting diedre line of:

22/5 Honest to God
42m S (4a) Forsythe and party, 1976
Follow the diedre on generous holds to the top, moving right across grass and rock ledges to finish. Belay on blocks at top of The Keep and scramble along the top to descent Great Gully.

22/6 Bird Leg Buttress
88m VS (4b,4c,4c,4a,4a) Curran, Kerr (two aid points), 1977; Smith (first free ascent), 1979
Start: This route follows the front of The Keep, starting at the toe of the Buttress just left of a prominent green groove.
1   18m Using a large flake, traverse left into the base of a groove and ascend. Exit left and continue to a large ledge on the right. Peg belay.
2   34m Move up and left around an awkward bulge. Continue up to a niche below a large overhang and traverse left until it is possible to gain the slab above. Trend right and upwards to a vertical crack overcome by jamming. Easier but exposed climbing leads to a thread belay behind a sloping ledge.
3   12m The large overhang above is split by an obvious crack. This is climbed with difficulty to belay above.
4   12m Easier climbing leads to a large ledge which is followed left. Climb a short diedre to an enormous grass ledge.
5   12m The final tower is climbed by the obvious diedre in its right-hand flake. Thread belay.

Index of routes by area

1 Dalkey Quarry

1/1	Pilaster 15m VS (4c)	25
1/2	Bushmills 12m HVS (5b)	25
1/3	Bracket Wall 18m VS (4c)	25
1/4	Charleston 15m HS (4a)	25
1/5	Mahjongg 12m HVS (5a)	27
1/6	Levitation 15m S (4a)	27
1/7	Paradise Lost 16m VD	27
1/8	Scavenger/Exertion 18m HVS (4c,5a)	27
1/9	D Route 24m S (3c)	28
1/10	E Route 24m VS (4c)	28
1/11	F Route 18m HS (4b)	28
1/12	Gargoyle Groove 15m HVS (5b)	29
1/13	Winder's Slab 11m HS (4b)	29
1/14	Winder's Crack 11m VD	29
1/15	Paul's Edge 12m HVS (5a)	29
1/16	Jameson Ten 14m VS (4b)	31
1/17	Calypso 14m S (4a)	31
1/18	Tramp 9m VS (4c)	31
1/19	Shuffle 9m HVS (5b)	31
1/20	Dirty Dick 9m VS (4c)	31
1/21	Central Buttress 22m E1 (5b,4b,4b)	35
1/22	Thrust 24m HVS (5a)	35
1/23	Preamble 23m VS (4c)	36
1/24	Giant's Staircase 26m S (3c)	36
1/25	Graham Crackers 20m HVS (5a)	36
1/26	After Midnight 18m E2 (5c)	39
1/27	Tower Ridge 40m D	39
1/28	Helios 34m HS (4b/c)	39
1/29	In Absentia 20m VS (5a)	41
1/30	Hyperion 21m HS (4c)	41
1/31	Erewhon 9m E1 (5c)	42
1/32	Streetfighter 12m VS (4c)	42

1/33 The Shield 15m E2 (6a)   44
1/34 Eliminate A 15m VD   44
1/35 Eliminate A Dash 17m S (4a)   44
1/36 Eliminate B Dash 14m VD   44
1/37 The Ghost 23m E2/3 (5b/c)   45
1/38 Stereo Tentacles 14m HVS (5a)   45

2 Glendalough
2/1   Cracks on the Garden of Eden 29m VS (4b)   47
2/2   Expectancy 21m VD   49
2/3   Quartz Gully 54m HS (3c,4b,3c)   49
2/4   Holly Tree Shunt 55m VD   51
2/5   Prelude/Nightmare 74m VS (4b,4b,4a,4c)   51
2/6   Spillikin/Fanfare/Speirbhean 83m HVS (4c,5a,4c)   51
2/7   Spillikin Ridge 86m E2 (4c,5c)   52
2/8   Sarcophagus 84m HVS (4b,5a,5a,5a)   52

2/9   Bruces Corner 21m VS (4c)   57
2/10 Celia 29m VS (4b)   57
2/11 Aisling Arête 28m VS (4b,4a)   57
2/12 Lethe 29m VS (4c)   59
2/13 Forest Rhapsody 110m VS (4c,4a,3c,4a,4a)   59
2/14 Ifreann Direct and Chimney 35m E1 (5a,5b)   60
2/15 Silent Movie 90m E3 (5c,5c)   60
2/16 Cornish Rhapsody 110m HVS (4c,5b,4a,4b)   63
2/17 Cuchulainn Groove 45m HS (4a,4b)   63

3 Luggala
3/1   Hyrax 54m HVS (4b,4c)   67
3/2   Caravan 50m E2 (5b,5b/c)   69
3/3   All Along the Watchtower 62m VS (4b,4a,4b)   71
3/4   Curved Air 80m VS (4a,4b,4b)   71

3/5   Stepenwolf 70m E1 (5b,5b,4a)   73
3/6   Muskrat Ramble 80m HVS (4b,5a,4c)   73
3/7   Silent Spring 45m HVS (5a,4a)   75

3/8   Pine Tree Buttress 92m S (3c,3c,3c,4a,3c)   75

3/9   Clingon/Claidheamh Solais 50m VS (4a,4c,4b)   77
3/10 Spearhead 60m HVS (4a,4b,4a,5a)   79
3/11 The Gannets 60m E2 (5c,5a)   79

3/12 Dance of the Tumblers 55m HVS (5b,5a)   80

4 Coumshingaun
4/1   Emperor's Nose 60m E1 (5b,5b)   83
4/2   Dark Angel 60m HVS (4c,5a)   85
4/3   Crooked Smile 60m VS (4b,4b)   85

4/4   Jabberwock 95m HVS (5a,4b,4b)   87
4/5   Gargantua 90m HVS (5a,4c)   89
4/6   Colossus 104m VS (4c,4c,4c)   89

5 Ailladie
5/1   Ground Control 16m VS (4c)   93
5/2   Atomic Rooster 16m HVS (5b)   93
5/3   Genesis 16m HS (4b)   95
5/4   Bonnain Bui 15m VS (4c)   95
5/5   Nutrocker 15m HVS (5a)   95
5/6   Rollerball 28m E2 (5c)   95
5/7   Gallows Pole 28m E2 (5c   96
5/8   The Marchanded Crack 28m E1 (5b)   96
5/9   Skywalker 32m E2 (5c)   96
5/10 Moments of Inertia 30m E3 (6a)   96
5/11 Box of Chocks 24m S (3c)   99
5/12 Promised Land 24m E1 (5b)   99
5/13 The Ramp 45m E1 (5b,5a/4c)   99
5/14 Pis Fluich 30m HVS (5a)   101
5/15 Doolin Rouge 25m HVS (5a)   101
5/16 Great Balls of Fire 26m HVS (5a)   101
5/17 Black Magic 26m HVS (5a)   104
5/18 Salt Rope 24m E1 (5b)   104

6 Monastir Sink

6/1	Mike's Route 20m VS (4b)	109
6/2	Spider 20m HVS (5a)	109
6/3	Monastir Direct 33m HVS (5a)	110
6/4	Black Bastard 27m VS (4b)	110

7 Tormore Crag

7/1	Ferdia 24m HVS (5b)	111
7/2	Above the Salt 27m E2 (5c)	113
7/3	Warthog 24m HVS (5b)	114
7/4	Halfbreed 24m HVS (5a)	114
7/5	Strongbow 24m VS (4c)	114
7/6	Condor 24m HVS (5a)	115
7/7	Weekend Warrior 30m E1 (5c)	115
7/8	Leda 27m E1 (5b)	115
7/9	Fergus 21m S (4a)	117
7/10	Sparrow 27m HVS (5a)	117
7/11	Mourne Rambler 18m E1 (5b)	117
7/12	Hawk 30m HVS (5a)	119
7/13	Maeve 18m VS (4b)	119
7/14	Deoch an Uasail 18m VS (4c)	119
7/15	Bedroom Boredom 24m HVS (5a)	120

8 Muckros Head

8/1	Scut 11m E2 (5c)	123
8/2	An Raibh Tu ar an gCarraig 15m	123
8/3	Bombay Duck 15m S (4a)	126
8/4	Tricky Dicky 17m VS (4c)	126
8/5	Cois Farraige 18m VS (4c)	126
8/6	Morning Glory 17m HS (4b)	126
8/7	The Barb 18m E1/2 (5b)	126
8/8	Boho Dance 20m S (4a)	128
8/9	Froth 18m HS (4b)	128
8/10	Primula 18m VS (4c)	128

9 Sail Rock
9/1   Main Mast 69m E2 (5b/c)   129

10 Malinbeg
10/1   The Bosun's Ladder 15m S (4a)   131
10/2   Hydrophobia 15m VS (4b)   133
10/3   Calvin's Corner 8m VS (4b)   133
10/4   Shiver me Timbers 20m S (4a)   133
10/5   Moby Dick 20m S (3c)   133
10/6   The Bold Princess Royal 30m HVS (5a)   135
10/7   Zimmerman Blues 30m VS (4c)   135
10/8   Lord of the Flies 25m HS (4b)   135
10/9   Flying Enterprise 27m HS (4c)   137
10/10   Fiddlers Green 27m HVS (5a)   137
10/11   The Wreck of the Mary Deare 27m VS (4c)   137
10/12   Pieces of Eight 20m E1 (5b)   138
10/13   John Dory 22m S (4a)   138

11 Lough Belshade
11/1   Byzantium 122m VS (4b,4a,4b,4a,4a)   139
11/2   Classical Revival 82m E1 (5b,5a)   142
11/3   Lest we Forget 75m HVS (4b,4c,5a)   145
11/4   Land of Heart's Desire 83m HVS (5a,5a,5b,4c)   145

12 Lough Barra
12/1   Diversion 133m S (4a)   149
12/2   Triversion 98m S (3c)   149
12/3   Lazarus 60m VS (4c,4a)   151
12/4   Gethsemane 84m E1 (5a,4c,4c,4c)   151
12/5   Aiseiri 109m VS (4c,4a,4b,4a)   152
12/6   Larceny 128m VS (4b,4a,4b,4b,4a)   152
12/7   Tarquin's Groove 108m HS (4b,4a,4a,4a,4a)   153
12/8   Surplomb Grise 136m VS (-,4c,4a,-,4b)   153
12/9   Rule Britannia/Erin go Bragh 79m HVS (5a,3c,5a,5a)   155

12/10   Calvary Crossing 84m VS (4c,4c,4c)   155
12/11   Ploughshare 62m VS (4c,4a,4a)   156
12/12   Fomorian 65m HS (4b,4a,3b)   156

13 Fair Head
13/1   December 55m VS (4c,4c)   159
13/2   Duais 42m E1 (5b)   159
13/3   Poor Relation 45m E1 (4a,5b)   159
13/4   Doldrum 72m E1 (4c,5b,4c)   161
13/5   Hurricane 63m E2 (5b,5b)   161
13/6   Toby Jug 55m E1 (5a,5b)   163
13/7   The Brasser 46m E2 (5c,5b)   163
13/8   Sandpiper 42m E2 (5c,5a)   163
13/9   Striapach 56m HVS (4c,5a,5a)   165
13/10   Jolly Rodger 68m E3 (5a,5c)   165
13/11   Sreang Scuab 45m E2 (4b,5b)   165
13/12   Burn Up 75m HVS (5a,5a,5a)   167
13/13   Born to Run 75m E4 (6a,5c,5c)   167
13/14   New City Allstars 66m E1 (5b,5b,5a)   169
13/15   Scarecrow 100m HVS (5a,4c,5a)   169

13/16   An Gobán Saor 90m E1 (5a,4c,5b)   171
13/17   An Bealach Rhunda 112m E1 (4c,5b,4a,4c)   171
13/18   The Vandals 57m E1 (5c,5b)   173
13/19   Easy Rider/Aifric 80m E2 (4c,5c,5c)   173
13/20   Bates Motel/Solid Mandala 72m E3 (5b,5a,5b,5b)   175
13/21   Roaring Meg 100m VS (4c,4b,4c)   175
13/22   Cuchulainn 78m E2 (5a,5c,5c)   175
13/23   Conchubair 60m E2 (5a,5c)   177
13/24   Blind Pew 60m E2 (5a,5b)   177
13/25   Mizzen Star 60m E2 (5b,5b)   179
13/26   Titanic 63m E2 (5b,5c)   179
13/27   Salango 60m E3 (5b,5c)   181
13/28   Equinox 60m E2 (5b,5b)   181
13/29   Wall of Prey 75m E4 (6a,5c)   181
13/30   Hell's Kitchen 66m HVS (5a,5a)   183

13/31 Ocean Boulevard 60m E3 (5c,5b)   183
13/32 Aoife 57m E1 (5b,5a)   184
13/33 Girona 63m VS (4c,4c)   184
13/34 Chieftain 70m VS (4b,4b)   185

13/35 Eithne Inguba 72m E1 (5b,4c)   185
13/36 Argosy 69m E1 (5a,4b)   185
13/37 Odyssey 66m VS (4c,4a,4b)   187
13/38 Dearg Doom 69m VS (4b,4c,4c)   187
13/39 Pyrrhic Victory 66m E1 (5a,5b)   189
13/40 Black Taxi 42m E1 (5b)   189
13/41 Mongrel Fox 42m E1 (5b)   189
13/42 Thunderhips 39m E1 (5b)   191
13/43 Fireball 39m E1 (5b)   191
13/44 Midnight Cruiser 36m E1 (5b)   191
13/45 Communication Breakdown 36m E1 (5b)   191
13/46 Railroad 36m E1 (5b)   193
13/47 Sabre Rattler 38m HVS (4c)   193
13/48 Fath mo Bhuartha 24m HVS (5b)   193
13/49 GBH 24m E3 (6a/b)   194
13/50 The Black Thief 24m VS (4b)   194
13/51 The Fence 24m VS (4c)   194
13/52 The Offence 24m HVS (5a)   194

           14 Ballygalley Head
14/1   Iky-Mo 15m S (3c)   195
14/2   Lucky Strike 28m HVS (5a)   197
14/3   Reprisal 28m VS (4b)   197
14/4   American Beauty 30m VS   197

14/5   Dirty Sox 33m VS (4b)   197

14/6   Vindication 30m HVS (5b)   199
14/7   Cat's Eyes 30m VS (4c)   199
14/8   Deadline 30m HVS (5a)   199
14/9   Kleptomaniac 30m VS (4c)   201

14/10 Star Spangled Banner 25m HVS (4c/5a)   201
14/11 Clearway 25m E1 (5b)   201
14/12 Harry 25m VS (4c)   201
14/13 Debbie 27m VS (4c)   202

Introduction to the Mourne Mountains

15 Lower Cove

15/1 First Corner 27m HS (4b)   208
15/2 Dot's Delight 39m HVS (4c)   208
15/3 Gynocrat 30m HVS (5a)   208
15/4 Aristocrat 35m HVS (5a)   211
15/5 Pillar Variant 40m S (4a,3c)   211
15/6 Brewer's Gloom 45m S (3c,3c,3c)   213
15/7 Praxis Direct 43m HVS (5b,3c)   213
15/8 Les Jeune Filles 30m E1 (5a/b)   213

16 Slieve Beg

16/1   Devil's Rib 54m VD   215
16/2   Shadowfax 40m E1 (5b,5a)   217
16/3   The Fiddler 97m HVS (4b,5b,4b)   217
16/4   Wabash Cannonball 80m VS (4c,4a)   218
16/5   Satanic Majesty 57m E2 (4c,5b)   218
16/6   The Devil's Alternative 68m E1 (5b,5a,4c)   220
16/7   Polo 27m D   220
16/8   Parallel Lines 40m HVS (5a)   221
16/9   Sweetie Mice 40m HVS (5a)   221
16/10 Mourne Maggie 58m HVS (5a)   221

17 Annalong Buttress

17/1   Thin Crack 25m VS (4b/c)   223
17/2   Warsaw Convention 27m VS (4b)   223
17/3   Spanish Flea 38m S (3c)   223
17/4   Springtime 46m S (4a)   223

18 Hare's Castle
18/1   Thin Arête 25m VS (5a)   225
18/2   Third Party 25m VS (4c)   225
18/3   Duet 25m VS (4b)   225
18/4   Hellfire Corner 22m HS (4b)   225

19 Spellack
19/1   White Walls 30m S (4a)   229
19/2   Mad Dogs 35m E5 (6b)   231
19/3   Mirror Mirror 40m E3 (6a)   231
19/4   Warhorse 40m E4 (6a)   233

20 Bernagh Slabs
20/1   Crooked Chimney 80m S (-,-,3c,4a,3c)   235
20/2   Grand Central 91m VD   235
20/3   Hypothesis 88m S (3c,4a,4a)   236
20/4   Crescent 88m VS (3c,4b,4a)   236

21 Pigeon Rock Mountain
21/1   Virgo 90m VS (4a,4b,4b,4b)   237
21/2   B Special 72m E1 (4a,5c,4b)   239
21/3   Lunar Wall 73m HVS (5a,4b)   239
21/4   Geraldine 69m E2 (4c,5c,4b)   239

21/5   Class Distinction 30m S (4a)   241
21/6   Faerie Flight 27m S (4a)   241
21/7   Nuclear Wheelbarrow 30m HS (4b)   241
21/8   Falcon 27m HS (4b,4a)   244

22 Eagle Mountain
22/1   Great Corner 94m HVS (4c,5a,4c,5a)   247
22/2   Lassara Grooves 70m HVS (4c,5a)   249
22/3   Surplomb Sundae 35m VS (4c)   249

22/4   Tullamona Cracks 35m VS (4c)   250
22/5   Honest to God 42m S (4a)   250
22/6   Bird Leg Buttress 88m VS (4b,4c,4c,4a,4a)   250